Prints
and how
to make them

Prints

and how
to make them:

GRAPHIC ARTS FOR THE BEGINNER

by Arthur Zaidenberg

HARPER & ROW, *Publishers*   NEW YORK, EVANSTON, and LONDON

For Selma
with love and appreciation

Contents

The Pleasure of Printmaking

This book is essentially a primer.

It would be pretentious of me to present you with anything else. However, I think it would be equally pretentious of anyone, no matter how great his experience or how fine his own work in this delightful field.

Every etcher, lithographer, woodcutter, or any of the other graphic specialists knows the joy of experimentation and discovery. The happy and daring artist knows the delightful accidents, quite apart from set ritual, which gave qualities to his work, unplanned and unscheduled.

The pleasure to be derived from printmaking is not that of following a formula to the inevitable "right" result. A teacher can only guide the student to the rudimentary steps which summarize the graphic processes. He may also impart, if he is a good teacher, some of his love of the graphic processes and stimulate the student to share his enthusiasm. From this point the student must take off into the infinite, that unbounded creative area in which an artist lives, freely and passionately.

The New Graphic Freedom

The release of the modern artist from the stuffy gloom of the great art academies of the Victorian past brought with it a fresh approach to the graphic arts as well as to painting and sculpture.

The slackening of rigid rules imposed by "print purists" and professors of techniques have opened vistas for experiment in both method and concept which were once taboo to the graphic student.

Innovations of any kind were considered beyond the permissible in the etching class of the not-so-roaring twenties.

Every tool was surrounded by a ritual of reverence for the graphic "master" who had taught generations of graphic students and written heavy tomes, forbidding to the eye and stultifying to free artistic growth, but so imposing that they became graphic-art bibles, not to be challenged. Equally inviolable were the laws governing the use of graphic-art tools.

The rules laid down by the "print purists" added to the shackles which the graphic tyro was forced to wear as a student and hobbled his subsequent career as a professional, exhibiting graphic artist. The purists were, and in some areas still are, the gentlemen who dictated just what is authentic graphic art, when an etching is not an etching, just exactly what is permissible lithography and what is not deserving of that name, what is a print and how much like its brother it must be to make it acceptable to the expert and suitable for the files of a museum print-room or precious-art specialist's collection of authentica.

Until the blessed recent liberation, the graphic student was an easy victim of the controllers. The tools of the graphic crafts are so imposing, so numerous, and so regrettably expensive that they in themselves frightened the beginner. Similar in appearance in some cases to surgical tools, their application at first approach seems to require clinical training.

It was relatively easy to convince the average art student that in order to be allowed to make prints one had to qualify and have proper credentials. As for "showing," the "print societies" were usually as impenetrable and remote as the Fifth Avenue clubs made so famous and forbidding by Peter Arno.

Bless the bully-boys of modern art. One may disagree with their personal art and their manners but they have struck the shackles off the students and driven most of the precious "experts" into their subterranean file rooms and vaults. The sharp lines between painters and graphic artists have been broken down, and refreshing shows of prints by vital artists, untrained in the conventional techniques of the graphic rules committees, have appeared in our museums and galleries. Every good artist is now a potential creative graphic artist without the need of cap and gown and diploma.

The methods of producing these prints are almost as varied and many as the number of artists who created them. Some of these methods will be outlined in these pages. The purpose is not so much the teaching of the personal methods but rather the hope that the stimulating effect of their daring and freedom will imbue the student with similar zest.

We will also outline the conventional techniques of the graphic arts and the use of the apparatus for printmaking. Great works have been done with these methods, and the disparagement of the professors and purists was not intended to apply to the fine graphic artists in the past or the ingenious processes invented by daring innovators of long ago.

Arthur Zaidenberg
1963

INTRODUCTION *by Letterio Calapai*

Although a number of books on the graphic arts have been published in the past several years, to my knowledge none has covered the major techniques in such concise form as this work by Arthur Zaidenberg. It appears at a time when more artists, and even amateurs, are involved in printmaking than at any previous period and when more people are learning what an original print is.

Among the evidences of this so-called "print renaissance" are the great numbers of exhibitions being circulated in the United States by the American Federation of Arts and overseas by the State Department's United States Information Agency. Graphic arts centers have sprung up in many parts of the country and are flourishing; for example, Pratt in New York City and Tamarind in Los Angeles. Schools and universities have added new departments to meet demands for instruction. There has also been a phenomenal increase of print sales at the galleries.

A number of factors account for this situation. Today's prints, larger than in the past, are as creatively explorative, dynamic, colorful, and vibrant as oil paintings; and they may be purchased for only a fraction of the cost. Many people have learned that they can afford to have original works of art in their homes, and the names of such printmakers as Frasconi, Baskin, and Peterdi are as familiar to the American contemporary scene as those of Miró, Picasso, Braque, and Rouault have been to the European one.

This flowering of printmaking is primarily due to the efforts of Stanley W. Hayter, who in 1927 established in Paris his Atelier 17. His influence, particularly in the plate media, has been felt by many of the most important artists of our time. His approach combined a deep respect for the discipline of the craft along with an experimental attitude. He re-evaluated and held in the highest esteem the engravings of Mantegna as well as the explorations of Hercules Seghers. In trusting the imagination, he saw the burin as "an engraver's tool—a kind of plough which goes ahead of the manipulator, in an exploratory and inventive way, and not behind him." Thus he stimulated a generation of artists and freed them from the hackneyed mannerisms of the etchers and engravers of the late nineteenth century. In the area of the woodcut, a significant contribution was made by a number of artists of Japanese and Chinese background who wedded the ancient and highly developed art of the Orient to contemporary Western approaches. A natural consequence of these influences was the impetus they gave to exploration and freedom in the lithographic medium.

What satisfaction can you hope to get out of this field of printmaking? First, it is a challenge to find out whether you can grapple with a knife and a piece of wood, or see the effect of acid biting a line in a metal plate, or translate a free form onto stone or silk. There is a physical involvement that can be all-consuming in the creation of something: a figure, an abstract, an image of fantasy. Then there is the suspense of making the print: the inking, the rubbing, the pressure on paper. And finally, there is the moment of climax when the paper is lifted and the work is revealed.

The atmosphere is charged with the excitement of seeing your first product of creation, and you will feel impelled to share the experience with others and learn their reactions. Has the message come through? Has the material left its trace and spoken? Has the acid played with those lines and open spaces? Does the grain of the wood show sufficiently? Now is the time for discipline to see the work through to its final state. Your reward will be the satisfaction of mastering a new means of communication.

This addition to Arthur Zaidenberg's work will, I believe, be of great value to anyone interested in learning about the graphic arts. He touches upon the historical highlights, including the early rubbings from stone and wood. His scope is broad, for he covers the fundamental processes and techniques as well as current explorations in new art forms. His emphasis on the importance of exploration is illustrated by his own unique contribution of an inventive method of using the monotype which allows for fanciful variations. In short, he drives home his conviction of the importance of balance between form and content. In the ultimate analysis, the work of art lives by its emancipation from visible technical ties and soars to its own spiritual heights by its conceptual power.

Prints
and how
to make them

"The Scribe," woodcut. *Kalendrier des Bergers,*
Paris, Guy Marchant, 1500.
Courtesy of the New York Public Library,
Spencer Collection.

The Graphic Arts

From the earliest recorded period of man's existence on earth he has used the "scratching" method of incising lines in stone, wood, metal, and bone to imprint his art language. It was the first "engraving" process and, until the relatively modern invention of lithography, the basic method of all graphic art.

In many countries where there exists low-relief or intaglio (incised) sculpture by artists of primitive and ancient times, the natives have long practiced the "rubbing" method of taking impressions from these sculptured drawings. These were obtained by smearing the raised surfaces of the decorated area with soot or pigment and covering them with paper or cloth. Then the back surface of the covering material was rubbed with a stone or any hard tool until an impression was "pulled" from the sculpture.

This was the first multiple-print graphic method and it is of truly ancient lineage.

While this simple graphic printmaking procedure did not give an *identical* reproduction of the art from which it was pulled, it did give a "reasonable facsimile." The reasonable facsimile is, in a sense, the true result of all graphic methods, from earliest wood engraving to present-day, very much improved printmaking methods.

In this respect graphic art must sharply differ from mechanical reproduction methods, so highly developed in these days. Reproduction aims at faithful copying of an original drawing or painting. Graphic art aims to create from a basic drawing an amalgam of that basic drawing and the specific virtues inherent in the graphic-art procedure. An engraving, etching, or lithograph is not a true reproduction. No two prints "pulled" from the block, plate, or stone are identical, because part of the creative process of printmaking is the printing itself. Each print pulled calls for individual handling, and the variations in quality and beauty are great. These variations are inevitable and desirable. Each print is a unique work of art, subtly and beautifully different from its fellows.

With the happy growth of public interest in art, collecting is no longer restricted to the millionaire or the museum; it is now common practice among people of modest means. As a result, graphic prints by fine artists are increasingly in demand. This accounts only partially for the growing interest of artists in producing them. The exquisite possibilities of the many graphic methods increasingly capture the imagination of artists, and they are creating splendid work.

In this book I propose to examine the classic graphic-art methods, most of which are still in use by many artists. But—and this is more pertinent to our time—I shall demonstrate the many new methods evolved through the discovery and availability of new materials and techniques which have greatly contributed to the ease and fluency of the artist, eliminating many of the tedious, complex, and costly technical processes of the past.

It has been my good fortune to evolve several unique methods of making graphic prints. In all modesty they may be claimed to open wonderful vistas to graphic artists. These will be explained and taught in full detail in these pages, and it is hoped that the students and artists who experiment with them gain as much pleasure as I do from their use.

It is a deep conviction of mine that the artist should not be hampered in the performance of his true function, that of creating, by time- and energy-consuming preparations for work. With this thought in view, every effort has been made to simplify the steps to the creation of graphic prints. The most direct methods have been explained and the minimum of materials and expense advised.

Although those who stress technique and the scientific approach may challenge some of these simplifications, they have been helpful to me, and I hope they may guide you to choose your own methods and media, and still leave enough scope for your own discoveries and tastes.

Rubbings

The earliest graphic art used as a means of reproducing calligraphy and drawings was that of taking "rubbings" of low-relief carvings on stone and wood, and transferring them to rice paper.

A thousand years before the Europeans were making woodcuts, engravings, and etchings the Chinese were making stone rubbings of legends and designs sculptured on flat stones. These sculptures had not been made to serve as a matrix for the rubbing but rather were bas-reliefs on temples and monuments.

Beautiful calligraphic letters, abstract designs of distinction, were carved in wood and on stone blocks, and "rubbed" reproductions of these were made in quantities for a literate public much advanced beyond the people of Europe.

Reproduced here are two examples of rubbings made from calligraphic characters and bound with others in a book. They were "printed" in the Han Dynasty as early as 200 B.C. and in the Tang Dynasty about 600 A.D.

Stone rubbing, calligraphy of the Han Dynasty, 202 B.C. to 220 A.D.

The ingenious would-be printer used the simple method of laying a sheet of rice paper over the legend in bas-relief or intaglio carving and rubbing the surface with a grease crayon, thereby registering on the paper a facsimile of the design beneath. Unlike the impression from a wood block or etched plate, the rubbing print was not in reverse. The rice paper facsimiles were distributed throughout the land in quantities not possibly obtainable from the more delicate blocks and plates.

Every child has at one time or another made similar rubbings by placing a sheet of paper over a coin and scribbling over the sheet of paper to register the coin's image.

While the making of rubbings can hardly be called creative graphic-art work, the fact is that rubbings in themselves are often beautiful and have only a similarity to the original.

Exquisite rubbings of fine bas-reliefs from Indian temples have become popular and they are distinctive art objects on their own. They are often made in various colors and the impressions are done with care and discrimination.

Examine the four reproduced and you will see that they are not mere reproductions of sculpture. They are works of art.

Stone rubbing, calligraphy of the Tang Dynasty 618–906 A.D.

Rubbings from Indian temple sculpture.

Essentially these rubbings are made by the same process as printed woodcuts and etchings but, since the carvings are stationary, no press could be used nor could the carved surface be inked without defacing the structure of which they were a part.

Other examples of the rubbing process.

The Block Print

The block-print process was introduced into Europe sometime around the end of the fourteenth century. Its values were more utilitarian than esthetic; it served as a purveyor of news, satire, and political propaganda as well as the interpretation of religious themes for a great population unable to read.

Movable type was still to be invented, but it obviously was inspired by the print block.

Long before this printing method was introduced in Europe, the print-rubbing methods had been highly developed in China and India.

To pull a facsimile from a bas-relief, the paper is placed against the clean sculptured surface and its back is rubbed with a flat-edged crayon or pencil. The image appears unreversed on the paper.

Subject and Medium

Artists are by nature experimental, on the lookout for original ways of expressing themselves. The creative process, by definition, implies unique expression of a thought or emotion. However, at the outset let us make one thing clear. More important than the finest medium of expression, the most skilled and individual technique, and the most expensive and delicate working equipment is the honest, personal statement of the artist.

Unless you have something to say with deep conviction after searching within yourself for your most profound conclusions, your keenest wit, your most intense excitement with which to say it, you will produce sterile, lifeless, meaningless scratches on paper. It will be a waste of material, time, and, most important, your potential as an artist.

The choice of the medium should always be based on consideration of the art statement to be made and the best manner of saying it. It stands to reason that if you wished to make extremely literal, detailed portraits of people, executed in a most realistic manner, you would not choose linoleum cutting as your medium. If you did so and despite the obvious drawbacks you succeeded, you would have performed a remarkable feat but you would also have violated the nature of the medium itself. Linoleum cuts have virtues intrinsic in the medium and those virtues are limited and valuable. Color woodcuts and etchings are valid and can be very beautiful, but it would be a serious mistake to try to achieve the same qualities and effects you would if you were using oils on canvas.

Each medium has special properties and, although experiments and daring innovations are often desirable and extremely successful, the essential nature of the medium must remain a contributing factor and not an obstacle to be overcome.

If time is available and curiosity intense, it is not unreasonable to try all media of expression. But the ancient axiom, "Art is long and life is short," unfortunately holds true, and creating is more important than exploring.

Until relatively recent times graphic artists were restricted to making small-size prints. The limitations were set by such arbitrary conditions as the size of the press rollers, the size of available stones and metal plates, and the conventions imposed by the "market." However, during the last few years, as technical facilities have improved and the demand for large pictures has increased, it has become possible to make prints of almost any size. This has enabled the graphic artist to expand the scope of his art statement; and the fine-line delicate tracery of old has given way to powerful expression in technique and subject matter.

Study the works of artists in the many graphic media shown in these pages and in the far more informative collections in the museums and galleries. Choose the method that seems most suitable for what you want to achieve, and concentrate on it long enough to decide whether it is the right technique to express what you want to say. If the method suits your temperament and work style, make it your own. Whims are fun but they can detract from steady progress. Many artists have found that it requires long practice and study to master any one of the graphic media and use it for increasingly satisfying results.

In the following pages you will find the basic principles of the main graphic media and a number of new ones.

Relief Cutting

When the lines and areas to be printed are cut to stand out from the flat surface of a block, the process is called relief cutting. For the most part this is the process used in making wood-block prints, wood engravings, linoleum cuts, and cuts using many of the new composition materials available for making prints in relief.

The Nature of Woodcuts

The chief characteristics of a good woodcut are strong contrasting values of black and white or colors executed with simplicity and having a special dignity not easily attainable in other media of art expression.

Although the medium is capable of being employed to express very subtle tonal values, as witness the delicate traceries of Chinese and Japanese wood-block prints, the essential quality is simplicity and bold contrast.

Black and White Woodcuts

One of the great virtues of the woodcut lies in its potential for sharp, contrasting forms of deep black against clean, sparkling whites. Even direct painting with black paint on white paper must of necessity lack the sharp edges and intensity of the solid black and untouched whites printed upon the paper under pressure.

Since the utilitarian function of the wood block was eliminated by the invention of photoengraving, the medium has resumed its purely esthetic place in the repertoire of media available to artists; and the range of experiment with its possibilities has widened in the Western world almost reaching the subtlety and daring of the Chinese and Japanese woodcutters.

Interesting and creative as these experiments have been, it is my opinion that the stark simple black and white contrast is the best use of the medium.

Here are the basic cutting and printing steps in making a simple black and white woodcut.

1. Buy a block in any artists' supply store. They can be made of maple, pear, or apple wood, or any of the many relatively hard woods. The grain of the wood follows the flat working plane.

2. The drawing can be made directly on the flat cutting surface with pen or brush and India ink. The final print will be substantially the same as the drawing except that it will be in reverse.

3. *Only the white areas are to be cut away* from the surface, the principle being that the remaining surface areas will be the ones which, when inked and subjected to pressure, will print.

4. *Cutting.* Gouge out the blank areas of the block to a slight depth below the flat surface with your cutting tool. When all of these blank areas are cut away, the block will be ready for inking.

5. *Inking the block.* Black printer's ink which is obtainable in tube form is used for this purpose. A generous gob of ink is squeezed onto one end of a slab of glass or porcelain or on a palette. A hard roller is used to "work" the ink to a thin consistency and during the process the roller becomes thoroughly covered with ink. Then it is passed over the wood block several times so that a thin but very black film of ink covers only the desired areas.

6. *Printing.* Most woodcutters "pull" the first few prints by hand rubbing. This is done by placing a sheet of slightly moistened (not wet or even too damp) paper on the block surface which is wet with ink. With a spoon rub the paper gently with a circular motion. You can watch the development of the printing process through the paper. (Use lightweight but strong paper.) When it is apparent that the entire inked design has been transferred to the paper your print is completed. You may safely peek at the print during the rubbing process by lifting an end of the paper carefully to see if the ink is transferring properly.

If after the first proof is pulled you feel that more work should be done, the block can be washed and dried and the cutting resumed. When the block is finished to your satisfaction the ink-rolling procedure is repeated and another print is pulled. The block must be re-inked for each print.

Small block printing presses which work on the pressure principle are available in the art shops. These are suggested if a large edition of the prints is desired.

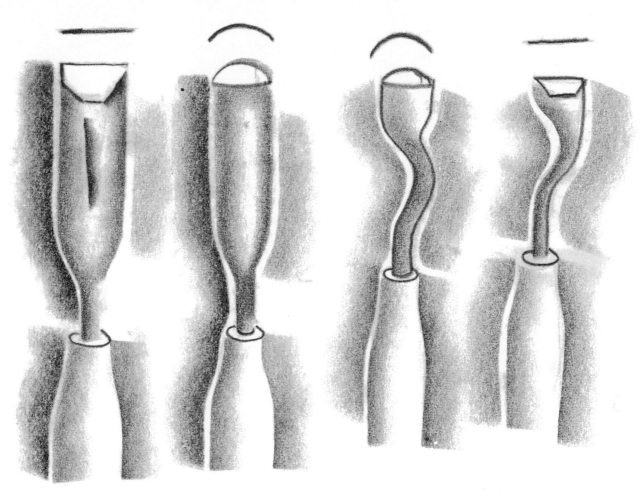

Woodcutting tools.

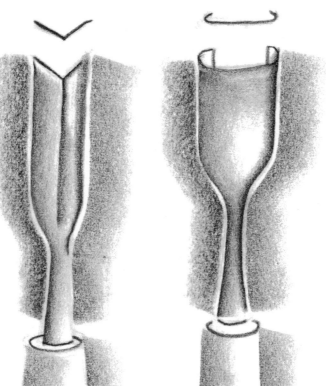

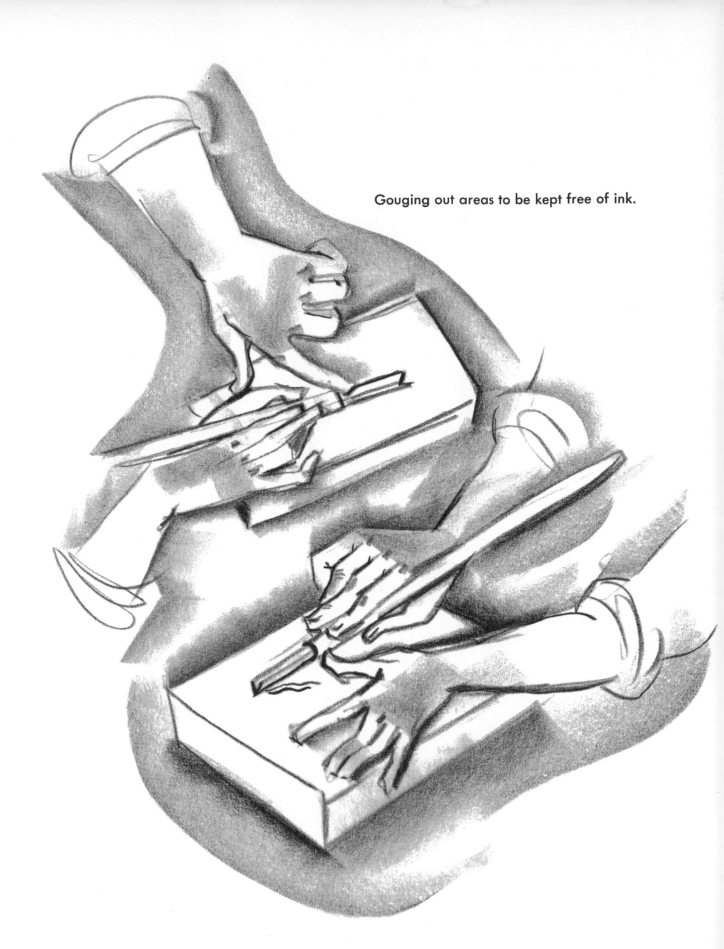

Gouging out areas to be kept free of ink.

Cutting.

Cutting a large area.

The special printer's ink used for rolling
on the plate, stone, or block.

Inking the plate.

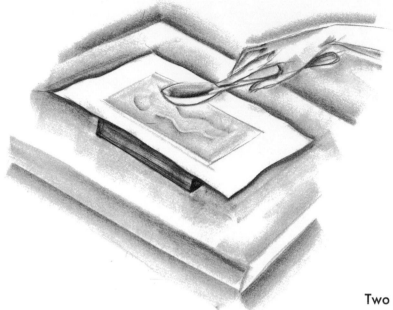

Two methods of rubbing.

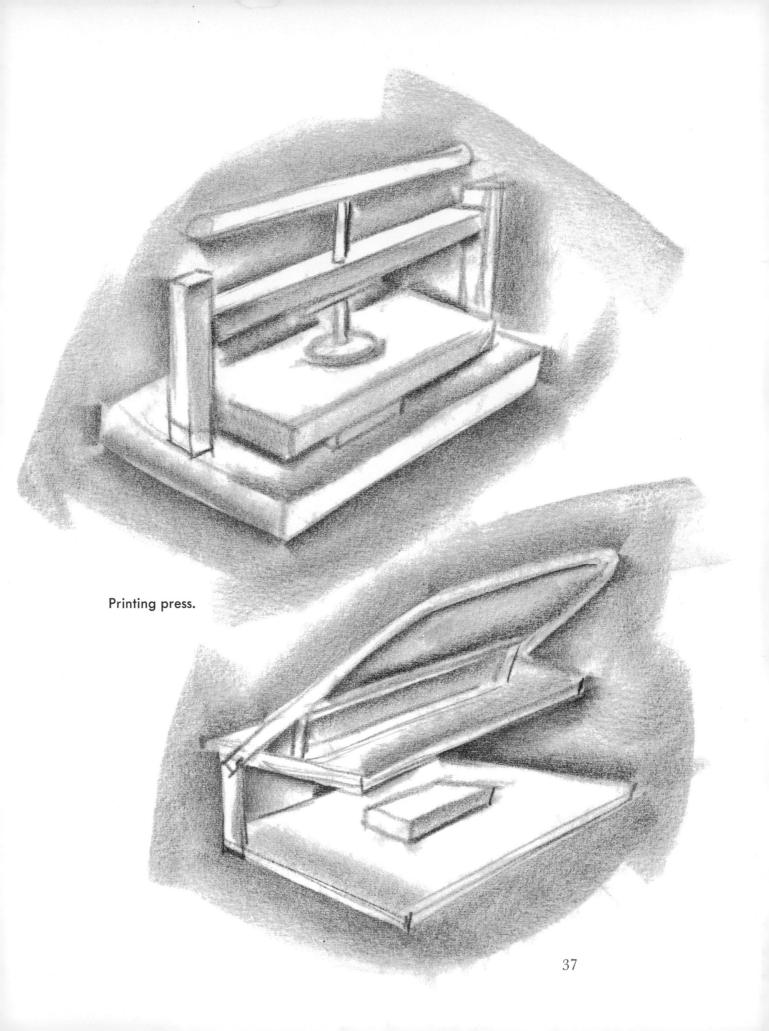

Printing press.

Making a woodcut.

Inking the roller.

Applying the ink.

Taking a look at the print.

The sketch.

Proof made from rubbing.

Proof after inking.

First proof.

Second proof.

Third proof.

"*Turrecremata Meditationes,*" Rome, Gallus & Simon, 1473.
Courtesy of the New York Public Library, Rare Book Division.

in der welt lyt wan als verr jerusalem von miozen landen lyt/also verr lyt es ouch von jndien das ober land heit wan es heist Orient das ist der sunnen pffgang/vnd das jerusalem mitten in derfi e/oz bewist da mit wen man pff den mittentag ein gleffi pffrichtet zu jerusalem so git sie keinen schatte pff die sitte/als sie tut in difen lande oz ist so tag vn nachtglich lang sind· vnd ouch zu jerusalem ist gar ein tuffi pfütz wer dar in steiget in der zitt des jars/ so tag vn nacht gleich seint oz die sonn glich ob im ist/vnnd da bp merckt man das jerusalem mitten in der welt sp/vnno des git ouch kunig dauio gezügnüs/da er spricht in dem psalter·Et operatus est in medio terre·Das ist zu tuisch Gott het pnser heil ge-

Detail of a page from Sir John Mandeville's
"Reysen und Wanderschafften durch das Gelobte Land,"
Strassburg, Johan Prüss the elder, 1483.
Courtesy of the New York Public Library, Spencer Collection.

"The City of Jerusalem," woodcut.
Breydenbach's *Reise ins Heilige Land.*
Mainz, Erhard Reuwich, 1486.
Courtesy of the New York Public Library, Spencer Collection.

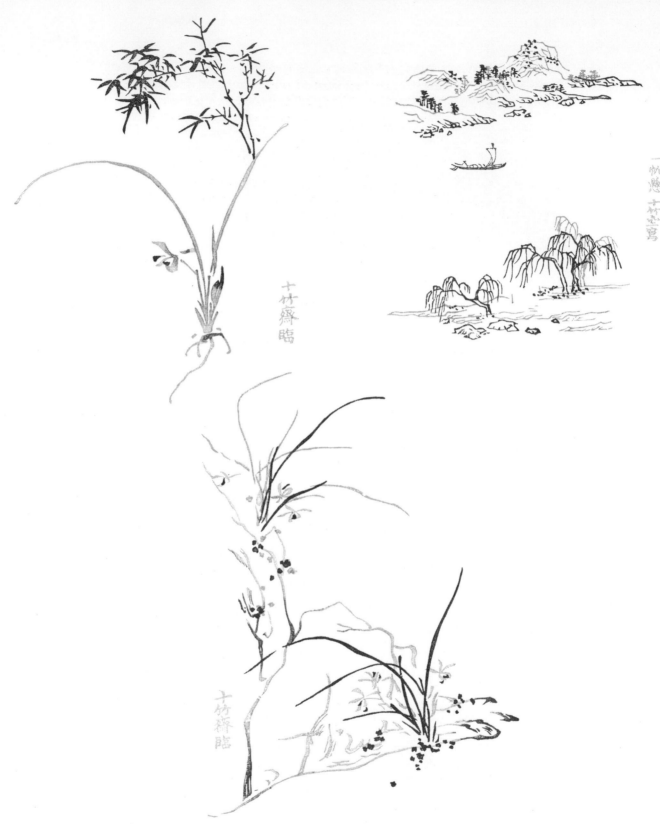

南平兩岸潤風正
一帆懸 十竹齋寫

十竹齋臨

十竹齋臨

Illustrations from Cheng Chen-To's *A History of Chinese Woodcuts.*
Courtesy of the New York Public Library, Prints Division.

44

Woodcuts from "*Macer Floridus De Viribus Herbarum*," Paris, 1503.
Courtesy of the New York Public Library, Spencer Collection.

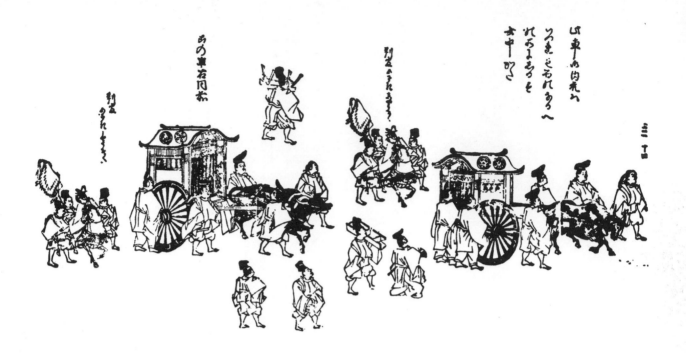

Woodcuts from *March of the Daimyo*. Japanese c. 1660.
Courtesy of the New York Public Library, Spencer Collection.

Wood-block prints.

"The Three Kings," by Karl Schmidt-Rottluff.
Collection, the Museum of Modern Art.
Reprinted by permission.

"Noa Noa," by Paul Gaugin.
Courtesy of the Metropolitan Museum of Art.

"Auti Te Pape," by Paul Gaugin.
Courtesy of the Metropolitan Museum of Art.

Making a Japanese Color Woodcut

The following pages will show the stages in the making of a color woodcut print by a fine Japanese craftsman and artist.

Not only were many colors used but even many variations of tonality and values within the colors. Some of the tonal variations were obtained by dilution of the inks used to create halftone values. Others were produced by variation of pressure in hand rubbing the print paper on the block.

Each color required a separate block and called for exact registration in printing. The final block was the tiny signature colophon of the artist. Japanese artists frequently used a drop of their own blood as the "ink" for that final block.

The order of printing is determined by the colors and spaces, *with the lightest colors and smallest spaces printed first*. The exact placing of each color in the proper space is obtained by the use of guides raised on each block. Watered color is brushed on the block, and then the face paper is placed on the block and rubbed with "Baren," which is made of bamboo sheath. This process is repeated for each block and each color. The intricacy of the technique will be apparent in the eighteen steps before the final print is achieved as illustrated in the following pages.

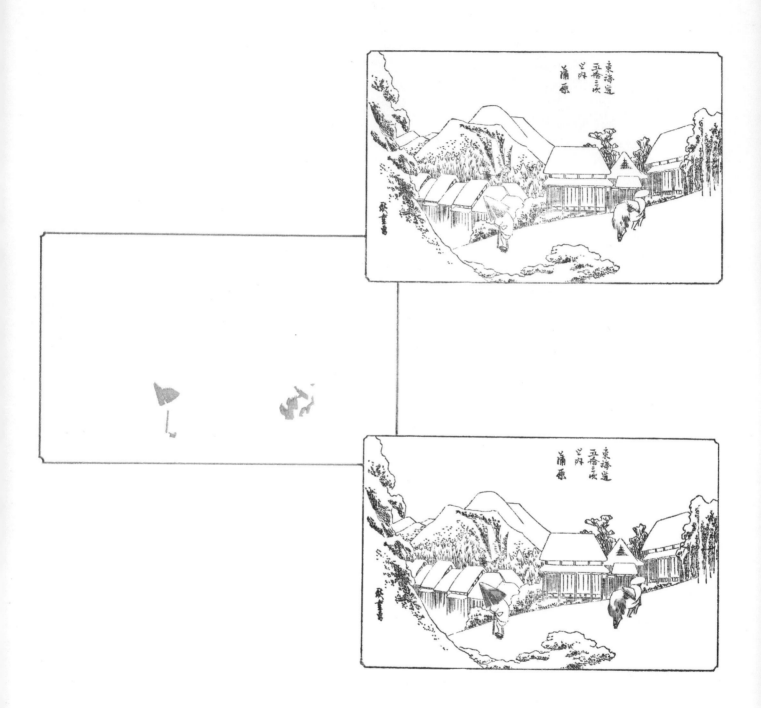

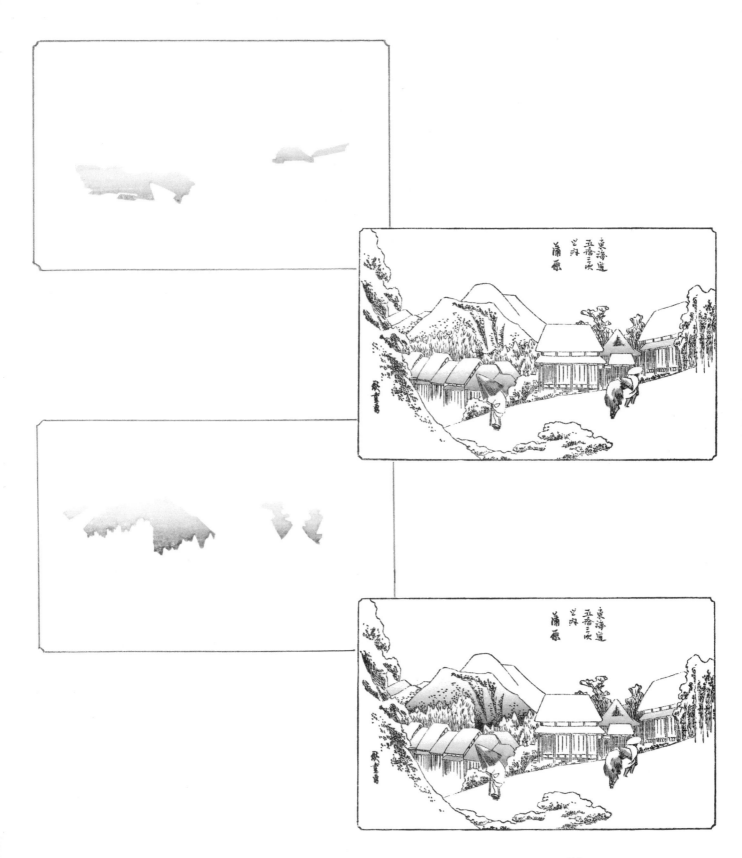

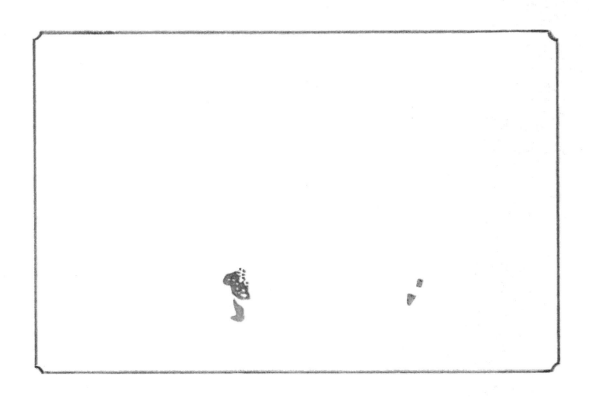

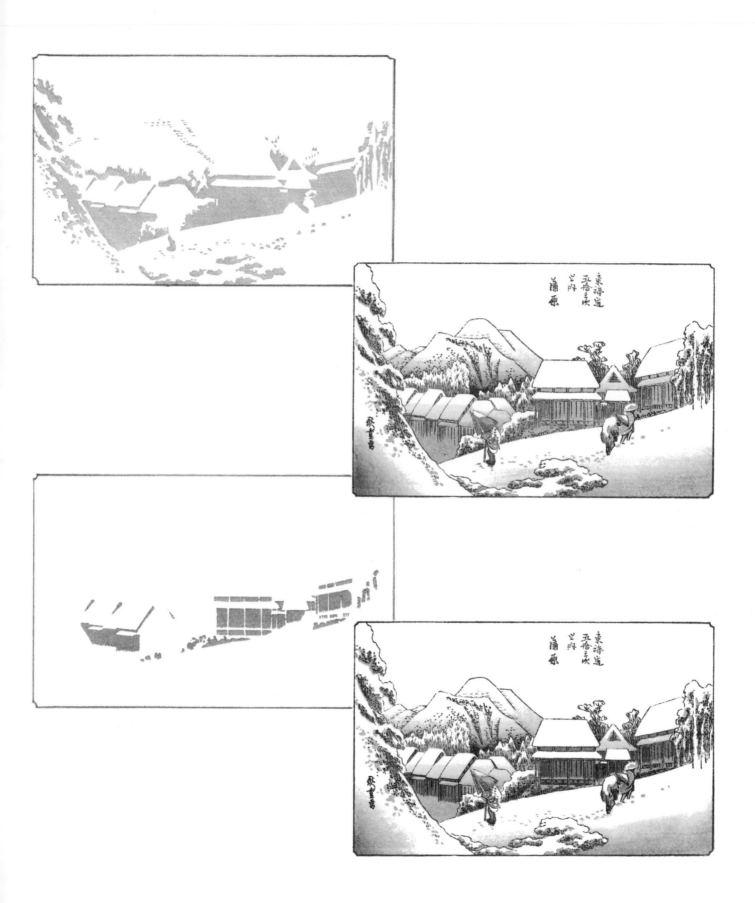

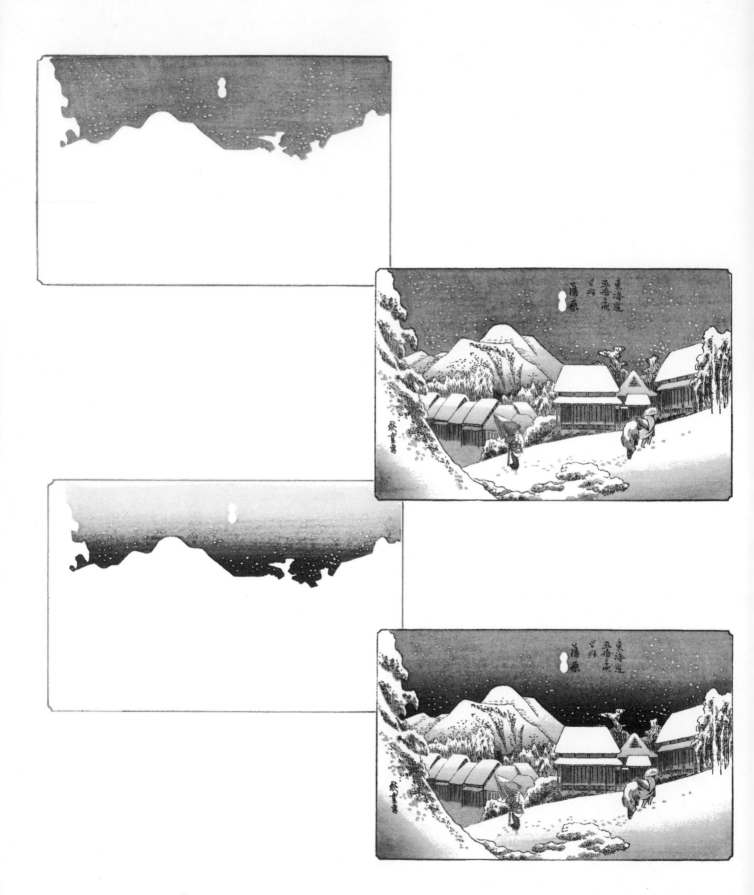

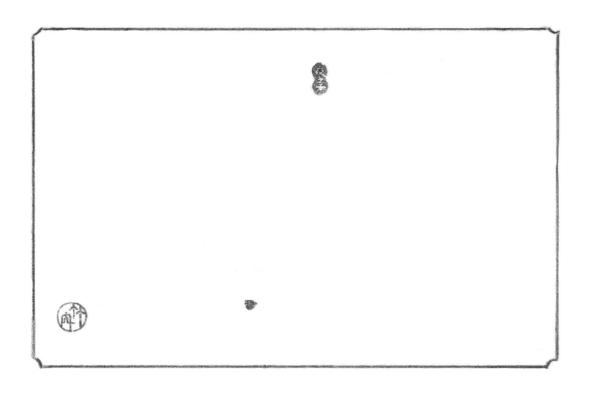

東海道
五拾三次
之内
蒲原

57

Wood Engraving

The essence of the process of wood engraving is the same as that of making woodcuts. The difference is one of terminology. The term "wood engraving" refers generally to work executed on hard, fine-grained wood. Very fine lines, close-cut, can be made on such wood. Boxwood, pearwood, and apple wood are the hardwoods commonly used for such fine engraving.

End-grain wood—that is, wood whose surface is composed of the tiny ends of the grain (as opposed to wood cut plankwise, with the grain)— is used for the finest wood engraving.

The cutting process and printing process are the same as those for making woodcuts, although finer blades and points are required for minute detail work and harder wood is essential to withstand the pressures of mechanical printing.

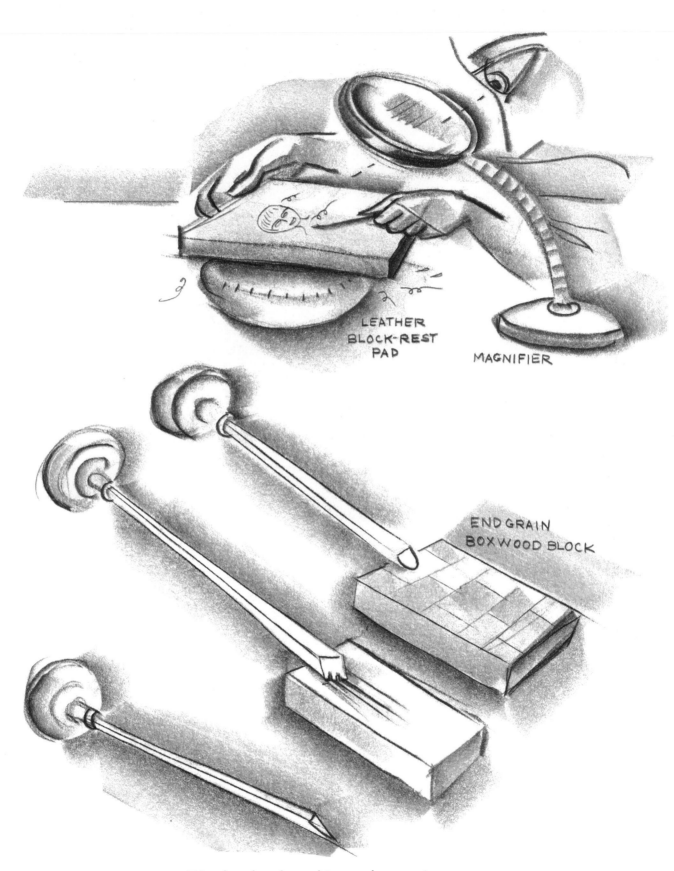

LEATHER
BLOCK-REST
PAD

MAGNIFIER

END GRAIN
BOXWOOD BLOCK

Wood and tools used in wood engraving.

Wood engraving by Alexander Anderson
(1775–1870) American. Courtesy of the New York Public Library,
Prints Division.

Steel Engraving

Steel engraving is, in the main, an intaglio process in which the incised line in a plate is filled with ink, which is transferred to the paper under pressure. The lines are cut only a fraction of an inch below the surface of the plate and when the ink is forced into these lines they print under pressure of the press rollers. The surface areas, having been wiped clean of ink, do not print. This is the basic procedure in steel engraving as well as in copper or zinc plate etching.

However, many fine steel engravings have been made in which the burin was used to produce "relief lines" as in woodcutting and wood engraving. Thus, although normally an etcher cuts in a line with the intention of having it print, the wood engraver incises two lines, one on either side of the surface. The same technique can be applied to steel, and has been used with good results, but hardwood lends itself better to the relief process.

In some cases a steel engraving can be cut in such a way as to form surface lines by cutting two below-the-surface lines so close together as to leave a thin surface line between them. When ink is rolled without forcing it *into* the incised lines, the surface line between them is printed under the press.

Linoleum Blocks

The principles of printmaking and cutting that apply to woodcuts apply as well to linoleum cuts. The work will inevitably be a little less detailed because the linoleum is relatively soft. It is advisable to plan a subject which does not require very fine lines. Most good linoleum which does not have the hard shellac finish will serve.

To cut the sheet to the size you require, mark the dimensions and score the lines with a sharp knife. The linoleum will break away cleanly.

The cutting tools are similar to those used for wood but need not be as finely tempered or as expensive. Good lino-cut tools are available in all art supply shops at a moderate price.

Linoleum offers little resistance to the cutting tools and there are no grain problems. This allows the artist considerable freedom, and spontaneous "drawing" can be cut right into the surface of the material.

An almost unlimited number of prints can be pulled if the block is not subjected to too much pressure in a press. Hand printing is preferable.

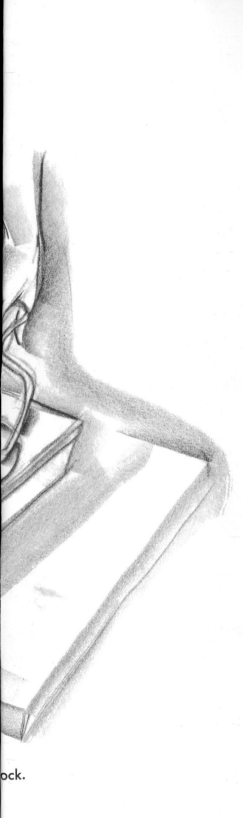

ock.

Linoleum block. Any good quality linoleum used for cutting in the process similar to woodcutting. The printing surface is in relief.

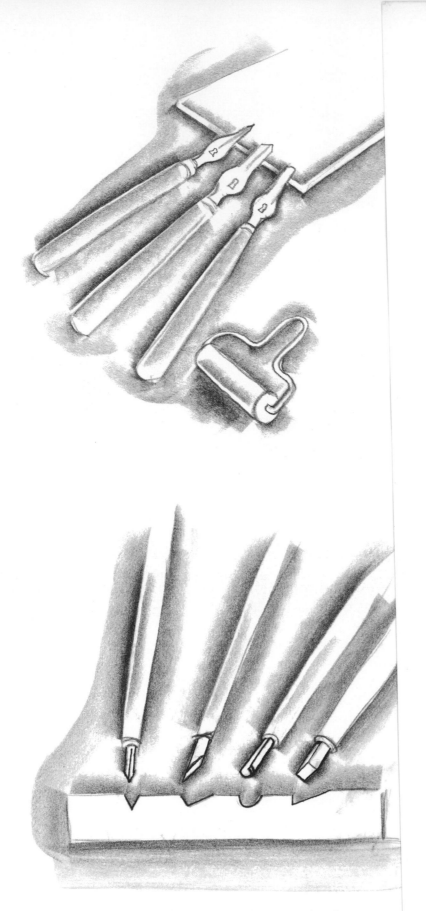

Special tools to achieve variety in shape of cut.

Inking the bl

"Lovers," by John McClellan, 1949.
Courtesy of the artist.

"The Kiss," by John McClellan, 1949.

"Sorrowing Woman," by John McClellan, 1949.

Incised Cutting

The process of sinking or depressing the lines and areas to be printed is known as incised or intaglio cutting.

The prints derived from incised cutting are the result of transferring to paper the inked incised lines under pressure of the press, the raised surface having been wiped clean.

In the case of etching, the incised lines are bitten into the surface of the copper or zinc plate by acids. In the drypoint process lines are scratched into the metal surface with a sharp-pointed tool. Metals and some plastic sheets may be used.

Steel engraving, etching, drypoint, mezzotint, and aquatint belong in this category.

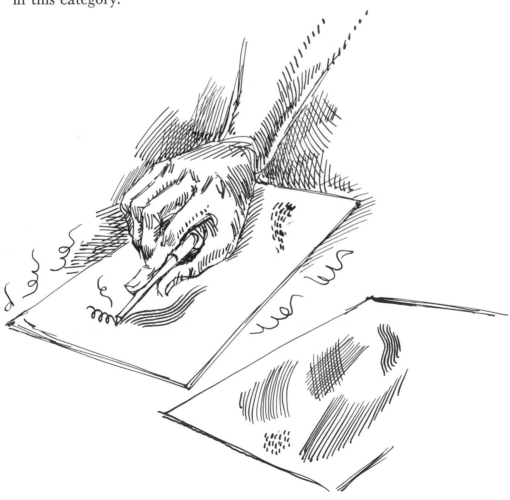

"The Printing of Books," by Theodor Galle (1570?–1633), Dutch.
Engraving from Jan van der Straet's *Nova Reperta*.
Courtesy of the New York Public Library.

New York, CA. 1627. This view appeared in
"Beschrijvinghe van Virginia, Nieuw Nederlandt," 1651.
Courtesy of the New York Public Library, Stokes Collection.

Drypoint

The beautiful, velvety lines of a drypoint print are the distinctive feature of the medium. Choose subjects where the play of freely drawn lines and small areas of gray tones produce the lightness and spontaneity so typical of this charming technique.

Drypoint is a relatively simple medium of graphic expression. Unlike its related medium, etching, no biting action other than the scratch of a pointed tool is required to penetrate the metal plate. The plate—copper, zinc, aluminum, or even plastic material—need not be coated with any preparation.

The tools are available anywhere. Where there is no art material shop stocked with commercial drypoint tools nearby, your dentist can probably be persuaded to give you old broken dental scrapers used for tooth cleaning. Sharpened (but not too much so) on an oil stone, they make excellent drypoint needles. Phonograph needles set in a wooden holder (a pen holder has served the author many times) can be used too.

It is nice to have diamond and ruby point tools if available. Drypoint tools with industrial jewel tips cut smooth grooves and throw up very little "burr," the ridge not unlike that which is thrown up by a plow in its passage through soft earth. The burr is sometimes retained if a furry line is desired, but if it is not wanted it can be removed with a scraper tool such as the one illustrated. This tool serves a double purpose—one end can be used to dispose of the unwanted burr thrown up by the drypoint tool; the other, called a burnisher, is for removing or reducing etched lines on a plate.

Drawing guide lines may be made on the plate with a pencil or transferred from a pencil drawing on paper slightly dampened and run through the press onto the plate.

Do not attempt to trace your pencil lines too slavishly with the needle point. The spontaneous character of the line is another desirable feature of drypoint, and this may be lost by such meticulous tracing.

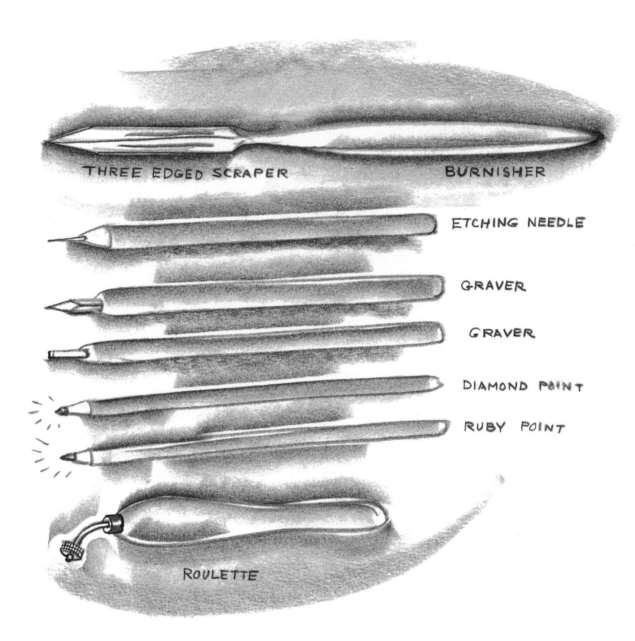

THREE EDGED SCRAPER

BURNISHER

ETCHING NEEDLE

GRAVER

GRAVER

DIAMOND POINT

RUBY POINT

ROULETTE

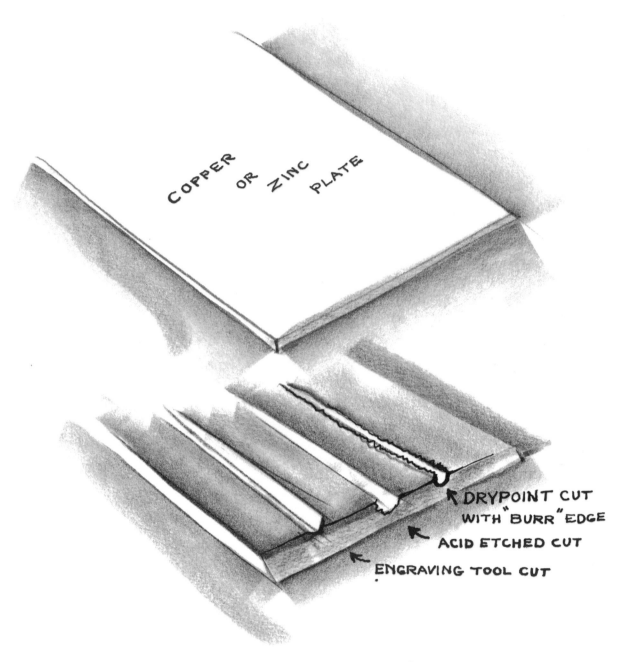

Burr. The metal ridges formed by the
cutting edge of the drypoint needle.

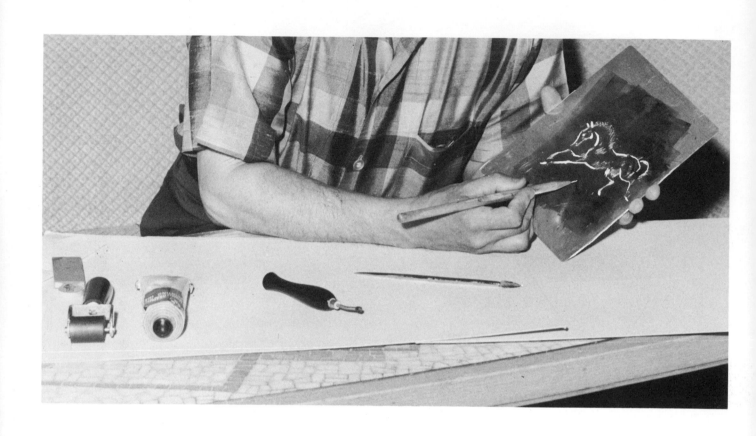

Drypoint on Celluloid

The advent of inexpensive synthetic materials has made easily available a supply of plastic sheets for use in the procedure known for a good many years as celluloid etching. It is a drypoint process, similar in almost all respects to drypoint etching on copper or zinc. However, it has two distinct advantages for the student that metals do not have: (1) the transparency of the plastic sheet, which allows the etcher to trace over a drawing, thereby eliminating a transfer process which is rather complicated and tedious on the metal plates; (2) the softness of the plastic sheets, which permits scratching with an ordinary mimeograph stylus or a needle point with comparative ease. Another advantage for some is the elimination of the unpleasant, chilling sound of metal points scratching metal.

One of the disadvantages of celluloid plates is that they must be handled with greater care than those made of metal. The very sensitivity which makes them easy to etch makes them equally subject to accidental scuffs and scratches.

On the whole, plastic is a satisfactory material on which to practice drypoint etching. It is light in weight, and its softness produces fewer true prints and calls for less refined, detailed drawing. In addition, plastic can be purchased almost anywhere and is considerably less expensive than zinc or copper plates.

Like so many of the less "classical" materials, celluloid etching is frowned upon by the purists; but to the student anxious to tell his art story with a minimum of obstruction occasioned by technical complications, this medium is recommended for the early stages of his drypoint efforts.

Procedure in Celluloid Etching

After he has chosen a subject, the student should make a sketch in some detail in either pen and ink or hard pencil.

It is advisable to use a thin tracing paper or any translucent paper because the print which results from any drawing made on a plate is always reversed (a disconcerting thing). Tracing on the transparent plastic plate from the reverse side of the tracing sheet drawing will produce a print that is an accurate copy of the original.

When you have made the drawing to be traced, turned it over, and placed it under the plastic sheet, you are ready to begin the drypoint drawing on your plate. It is advisable to tack the two (paper and plate) to a drawing board to prevent shifting.

If you want to check the progress of your drawing during the tracing procedure, slip a sheet of black paper between the plate and the drawing. This will throw the scratched lines into relief against the black paper.

Now begin to etch the drypoint lines with a stylus or needle point, following the lines of the drawing beneath. Use very little pressure. Any incised line, no matter how fine and shallow, will hold sufficient ink for printing. Very lightly impressed scratches will produce the finest lines and, of course, the greater the pressure on your tool, the deeper the cut lines and the heavier they will be when they are printed.

The most effective incision on a plastic plate is produced by holding the cutting tool almost upright, as in the illustration on p. 78. This will cut a V-shaped groove that is most receptive to the inking process and best suited to withstand the pressure of the press during printing.

As you become familiar with your scratching tools, whether you use a stylus, needle point, or a knife point, you will soon develop a technique of your own most suitable to your purposes. The illustration on p. 78 shows lines and combinations of lines that can be used to create areas of tone on the plate. You must, of course, remember that lines too close together or areas so deep and roughly cut as to be ink traps will result in uncontrolled blots on your print.

The celluloid or plastic sheet usually has squared-off edges. These sharp edges will cut through the print paper under the pressure of the press rollers. They must therefore be beveled to a gentle slope, away from the worked surface of the plate. This bevel may be made with a fine file, slanted as shown in the illustration. After the filing is completed, reduce the roughness of the edge with fine sandpaper, being careful not to scratch the etched surface of the plate.

When the bevel is clean and even, the prints pulled will have the characteristic plate-edge line typical of an original print.

Your plate is now ready for the inking and printing processes, which are exactly like those used in the etching and normal drypoint methods.

Hold the cutting tool upright for celluloid etching.

Kinds of lines to produce varying tones.

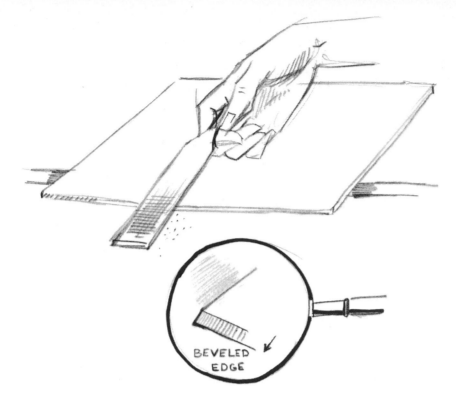

Filing a beveled edge on celluloid plate.

Drypoint on plastic or celluloid.

Etching

The art of etching is, by its very limitations, an exquisite one. Because of the essential nature of *line,* the thread of which all etchings are woven, this beautiful medium differs from all others except its closely related sister medium, engraving.

In ordinary drawing the decision to use line with pencil or pen is a voluntary one. The broad tone, filled in completely in various densities, is subject only to the whim of the artist. Of course certain variations from the pure etched line are also possible, but these are obtained only in the "biting" of the copper or zinc plate with acid or the "inking and wiping" in printing. The drawing made on the metal plate is restricted to fine line scratches and the variations of tone obtainable by combinations of lines in close juxtaposition, crosshatched and intertwining.

These limitations make the etcher's needle as delicate an instrument as the surgeon's scalpel and call for similar respect and dexterity in handling. Corrections of mistakes are laborious and not always possible without permanent injury to the plate.

Sensitivity of touch and purposeful decision in the use of the needle are imperative for the effectiveness of the print. The foregoing admonition sounds menacing. It is not intended, however, to frighten away the would-be etcher but rather to instill respect for a fine medium capable of being the vehicle for expressing the subtlest artistic emotions.

Briefly stated, here is the way etchings are made:

The Etching Press

Until relatively recently, etching presses were huge, heavy machines requiring special, sturdy benches and reinforced flooring to support them. However, small heavy-pressure presses, which are capable of producing very satisfactory proofs, are now available. The etcher who wishes to pull proofs wherever he may be can even buy a portable press for this purpose, but these are expensive.

There are, of course, expert professional printers who will pull a complete edition for a price. They are few in the United States, although there are some good ones. In France there are still a good many expert printers of graphic arts although the tribe is dwindling and the prices mount. However, the tyro etcher who uses this book can learn far more about the medium and its range of possibilities by doing his own proofing and running his own editions. In fact, a great many of the finest craftsmen of etching and lithography prefer to make their own prints on their own presses. It is part of the creative process, as you will discover in doing the ink "wiping" and in regulating pressure of the rollers to suit your purposes.

A good press should have smooth rollers, its traveling "bed" should have steady and even motion, and it should have pressure regulators which will allow for perfect balance and even distribution of pressure over the plate.

The plate lies on the board of the traveling bed; this board must be planed absolutely level and smooth. After the dampened paper is laid upon the plate, it is covered with one or two blankets of heavy flannel. These act as buffers between the metal plate and the roller. These flannel blankets are considered part of the press.

A metal plate (copper or zinc) is coated with a fine film of wax. A needle point set in a handle is used to draw the design on the coated surface. The point penetrates only the wax, exposing the metal beneath. When the plate is immersed in a bath of acid the lines exposed through the wax protection are "eaten" into the metal.

After this "biting" process the wax coat is removed and the printing ink is tamped into the bitten, incised lines. The ink is wiped from the surface.

The plate is then run through a roller press with a sheet of dampened paper covering its surface. The pressure of the rollers transfers the ink from the incised lines to the paper, producing a clean print. The inking, wiping, and printing process is repeated as many times as the relatively soft metal of the plate will permit without deterioration.

The variations of technique implicit in this outline of procedure are as many and as personal as the handwriting, thoughts, and emotions of the user. Add these differences to those of timing of the acid immersion, the biting power of the acid, quality of the inking and wiping methods, as well as variations of the pressure of the press rollers, and you will see that no two etchers can produce remotely the same character of print. In fact no etcher can produce identical prints from his own plate!

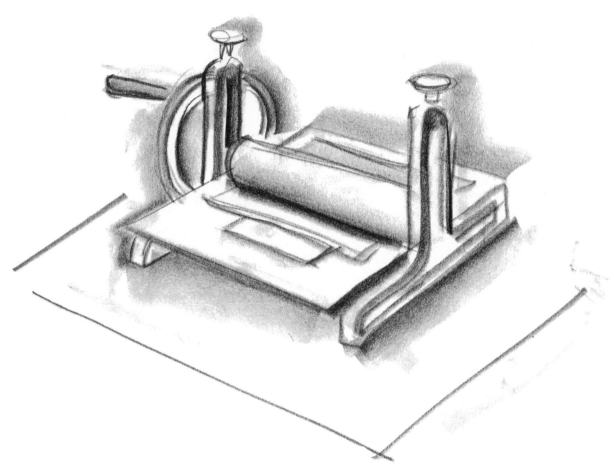

The etching press.

Etching Grounds

The protective ground for the first stage of an etching is composed of a thin film of wax spread over the working surface of the metal (copper or zinc) plate.

Etching ground wax can be bought in art supply stores in the form of hemispheres. Insert one in a silk bag, which is easily made. Then heat the plate over an electric hot plate until it is hot enough to melt the wax. Rub the bag of wax lightly and quickly over the heated surface of the plate, creating a semifluid film which can be distributed evenly with a roller or dabber made of leather.

Be sure there are no imperfections or porous areas in the wax film. A properly applied ground will be sufficiently thin to allow the free passage of the needle-pointed etching tool through its surface; it must also be even enough and adhesive enough to resist the biting action of the acid bath, permitting the acid to act on the exposed lines alone.

The Roller

A ground-laying roller is a fine and subtle tool. Because a ground must be strong and impervious to the action of the biting acid, it must be even and smooth. It must also be thin enough not to throw up a furrow as the needle point passes through it. The etching roller has evolved, through experiment, into the ideal distributor of such a film of ground. It is made of a revolving tube of wood covered with thick flannel to give it resiliency. This in turn is covered with heavy, smooth leather. It has a wooden handle on each end, and is handled like a rolling pin.

This delicate tool should be kept free of dust by storing it in a covered container with rests for the two handles so the roller portion will be suspended when not in use.

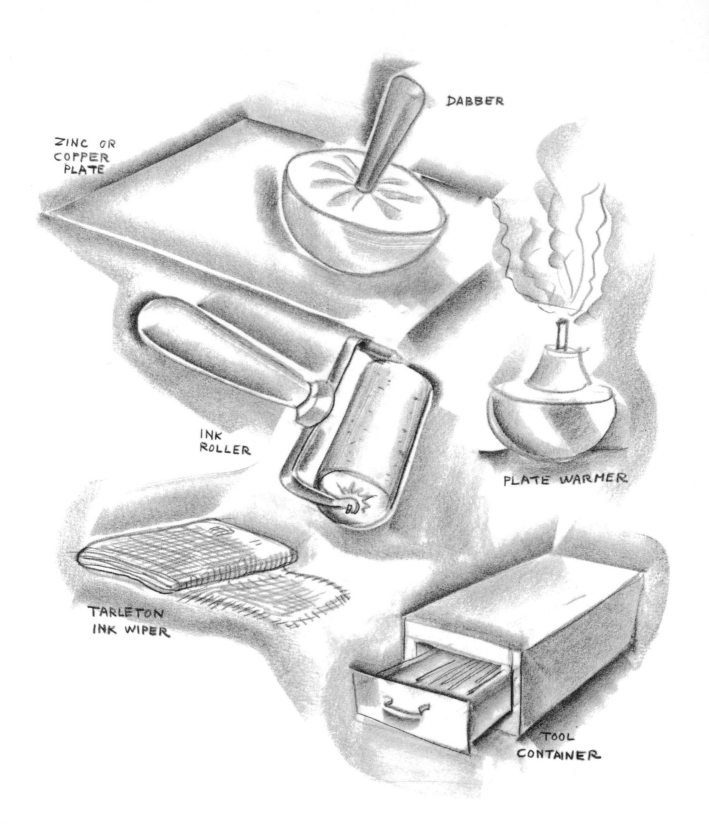

ZINC OR COPPER PLATE

DABBER

INK ROLLER

PLATE WARMER

TARLETON INK WIPER

TOOL CONTAINER

84

A hot plate for warming metal plates before applying ground and inking.

Wax grounding.

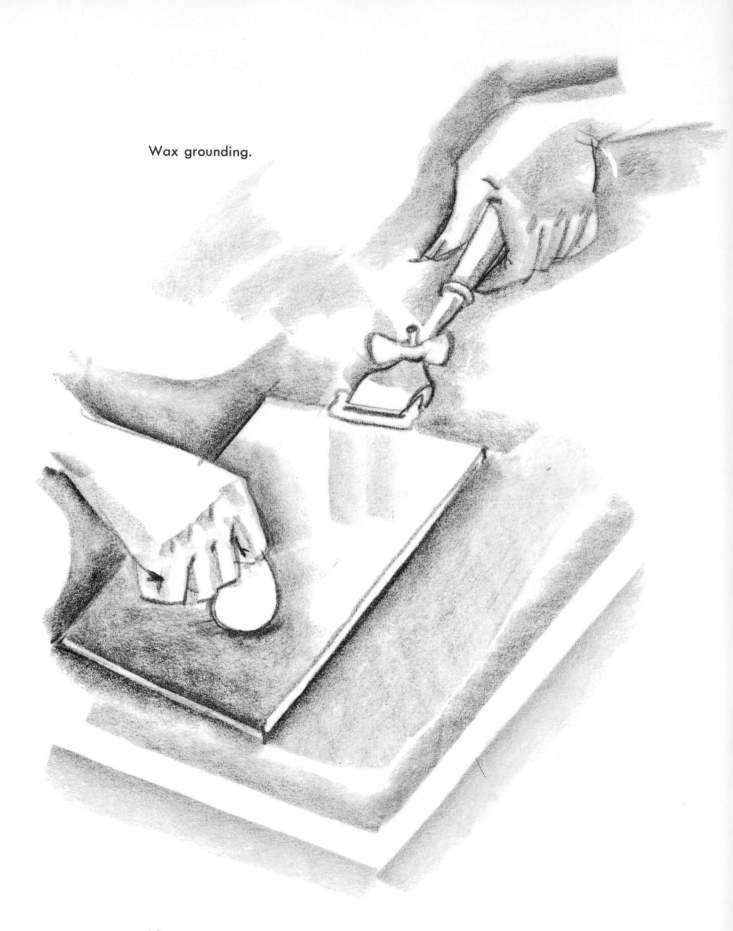

Drawing through the wax ground with the needle point.

Biting the Plate

The degree of light and shade in the print depends upon the depth and width of the line etched into the surface of the plate. Pressure on the etching needle has no bearing on this as the needle merely scratches through the wax film ground covering the plate. The character of the line is determined by the length of time it is exposed to the biting action of the acid bath.

Lines intended to be lightest in the finished print are bitten first. The first immersion in the acid bath should usually last fifteen to twenty minutes, depending on the artist's wishes. The plate is then removed from the acid and washed with clear water under the tap. The parts sufficiently bitten are covered with stopping-out varnish applied with a brush.

The plate is now immersed again for another twenty minutes. As before, it is removed, washed, and these areas are covered with stop-out varnish.

The next (usually final) biting should last between twenty-five and thirty-five minutes, depending upon the artist's purposes.

After the third biting the plate should be prepared for pulling the first proof. The acid is washed off under the tap; the wax is removed with a solvent. Turpentine can be used for this purpose. The plate is now ready for inking.

Stopping Out

The stopping-out process consists of covering areas that have received sufficient time of biting in the acid bath. This is done by brushing on varnish to protect these surfaces from further exposure to the acid. Then areas requiring further acid treatment can be immersed without risk. This stopping-out process can be repeated three or four times during the making of an etching before the proof print is pulled on the press.

Commercially prepared stopping-out varnishes are sold in etching supply art material stores. The entire back of the plate and the beveled edges should be protected with stopping-out varnish to prevent the action of the acid upon those surfaces.

Underbiting

It is very much safer to underbite a plate than to overbite the dark areas.

It is true that lines too deeply bitten may be reduced with the burnishing tool, but it is an uncertain process at best and calls for great care and dexterity with the burnisher.

An underbitten area may be rebitten after the first proofs show the need for deeper biting. However, when the lighter areas of a plate are underbitten it is most difficult to rebite, because when the ground is reapplied the faint lines may easily become clogged with the ground and cannot be revealed for rebiting.

The Bath of Acid

The acid bath most commonly used for the biting of a copper plate is composed of nitric acid diluted with water in equal parts. The mixture may be used a number of times and may be kept sealed in a bottle for a long period without deterioration. It is advisable to use either plastic or rubber gloves in handling the plate in the acid.

You will need a Pyrex dish sufficiently large to accommodate the plate, with ample space for its easy removal after each immersion. The dish must also be able to withstand the heat of an electric warmer—to about 90 degrees Fahrenheit. Some types of composition pans used for photography are acceptable as acid bath containers, but most will be affected by the action of the acid.

The sides of the dish must be sufficiently high to prevent the acid bath from spilling over, but not high enough to impede the quick and easy handling of the plate.

The depth of the acid mixture need be only slightly greater than the thickness of the plate.

Nitric acid. A biting agent most commonly used in etching.

Spreading Acid with a Feather

Some etchers who love to sketch spontaneously on the plate, unrestricted by the confines of the studio and the elaborate equipment, like to use what I shall call the "spit and feather system."

The already grounded plate, carefully protected against scratches by being slipped between the pages of a sketchbook, is carried about ready for the quick inspired sketch to be drawn and etched on the spot.

The needle-drawing aspect of the process is the same as that which is performed in the studio, but the biting acid is applied quite differently. Human saliva has a property of special interest to the etcher. For reasons unknown to this author, saliva spread over a limited area of the etching plate with a feather will confine within its boundaries any other liquid added to it in small quantities.

The etcher who wishes to bite his plate without immersing it in the pan of acid may pour prepared etching acid into the magic area of the spread saliva a little at a time. If the plate is held level, the acid will be restricted within the borders of the saliva and bite the plate only in that area.

The various degrees of biting may thus be obtained without stopping out, because the feather "spreader" will allow you to "paint" an acid-limiting boundary around the areas you desire bitten, and the application of the acid in small quantities controls the extent of the biting within the boundary.

Not a "nice" method, but less unpleasant than licking envelopes or stamps, the results justify the means, and this process gives an immediacy to the sketched etching unobtainable in any other fashion.

After the plate has been bitten area by area as desired, it is wiped clean with a fine rag. Then it is ready for removal of the ground and the application of the ink for pulling the first proof.

Inking for Printing Etchings

The inking process is not a difficult one, but it must be performed with care. Since only such lines as are thoroughly filled with ink will print cleanly and with their proper depth of tone, it is obvious that the leather-covered dabber must be used with some skill. The plate should be heated to a point where it is uncomfortable to the touch of the bare hand. (Of course you will be handling the plate with either rubber gloves or a hand vise.)

The inking plate should also be heated. When both are prepared, take a palette knife and spread a long dab of the warmed ink on the plate, distributing it evenly with a rotating motion until the entire plate is covered with ink. Use some hand pressure to direct the surface ink into the etched lines. You may also use your fingers to press ink into lines.

When the plate is thoroughly covered and you feel that the lines are filled with ink, you can begin the wiping process. Traditionally, etchers have used tarletan, a net cloth of fine texture. Its mesh picks up the heavy surface ink and, if properly used, leaves a fine film of ink on the flat surface of the plate. This film, regulated to the tonal quality of the author's purpose, gives the warmth that is characteristic of a good etching print. Other wiping cloths can be used if they are fine enough not to risk scratching the sensitive plate surface.

Other indispensable adjuncts are the side and heel of the right hand. Both are irreplaceable as sensitive wiping tools. This hand wiping allows for delicate variance in the surface ink film and does not remove any ink from the incised lines.

The inking and wiping process must be repeated for each proof pulled.

Tarletan. A mesh rag used for wiping excess ink from the metal plate surface after the ink has been forced into the incised lines.

Warmed ink being spread for saturating roller.
You may want to use rubber gloves.

Pulling the proof.

The Print Edition

The size of an edition of prints is limited only by the number that can be pulled before any deterioration of the block or plate results from pressure of the press or hand rubbing. To limit the edition for any other reason is either snobbery or commercialism.

An artist who has produced a beautiful plate should allow the widest possible dissemination of the prints. Gallery owners too often persuade graphic artists to make small limited editions in order to keep the price up. The loss entailed to art lovers is obvious.

Prints should be numbered as they are pulled from the plate, and the size of the edition should be indicated as well.

It has often been the procedure to destroy the plate after the edition is run. This has always seemed to the author an act of vandalism. Not only is it possible to rework the plate in most cases to the point of its original freshness but often it is still possible to pull quite good proofs only slightly less fresh than the first batch. If this "second edition" is so labeled there can be no question of unethical behavior involved.

"The Nativity," engraving, by Albrecht Dürer (1471–1528), German. Courtesy of the New York Public Library.

"The Month of January," etching, by Adriaen Collaert.
Courtesy of the New York Public Library.

"Landscape with Wooden Bridge," (B. 76), etching, by
Augustin Hirschvogel, (1503–1553), German.
Courtesy of the New York Public Library.

"Versailles, La Ménagerie," by André Dunoyer de Segonzac.
Courtesy of the Boston Public Library.

"Les Haleurs," by Jacques Villon.
Courtesy of George Binet Gallery.

Mezzotints

The prefix "mezzo" means half or middle, and this describes the quality obtained by the action of a rocker tool and a scraper on the surface of the copper plate. No acid is used.

The rocker is held upright, rocked back and forth, and at the same time propelled across the plate by gentle pushing.

The rocked plate would print an even black tone. By use of a scraper, various tones are worked out by scraping off areas of the rough burr produced by the rocker. The resultant prints are similar in appearance to charcoal drawings, but the effects are considerably richer.

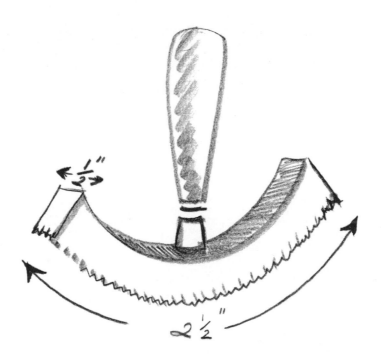

Mezzotint rocker, made of steel, with
many sharp teeth to bite into
plate and produce a textured surface.

Soft-Ground Etching

In soft-ground etching, ordinary etching ground is mixed with tallow before it is spread on the plate in the conventional manner. The tallow serves to soften the ground.

In the next step a fine sheet of tissue paper is placed over the plate. A drawing is then made on the tissue with an ordinary lead pencil, using ordinary pressure. When the tissue paper is lifted from the plate the softened ground will adhere to the tissue wherever the pencil has pressed.

The plate is then acid-bathed, inked, and printed in the usual manner. The results are warm tonal effects especially characteristic of soft-ground etching.

"The Mill Stream," mezzotint, by Fredric Reynolds.

Aquatint

Aquatint is a tonal process of etching rather than a line process.

In this method, a plate is covered with a finely powdered resin and the tones are produced by the stopping-out process.

A variety of aquatint is also produced by the sand grain method. A plate with an ordinary ground is covered with a piece of fine sandpaper and run through the rollers of the etching press. The tiny holes pressed through the ground will produce a fine-toned effect when subjected to the acid bath.

"The Quiet Street," aquatint etching, by John Taylor Arms.

"The Lotus Eaters," by Barbara Neustadt, Odyssey Series.
Courtesy of the Ruth White Gallery.

In "The Lotus Eaters" Miss Neustadt has used two plates. The first was prepared by rolling an over-all tone of light yellow on the plate surface with a roller made of gelatin. The ink itself was mixed with a gel which adds a transparency to the color. (This substance is obtainable at any well-equipped art supply store.)

The plate was then run through the press for the entire edition, leaving a yellow background on each sheet. Plate 1 had now served its purpose. The second plate carried the etched, engraved, and aquatinted areas of the picture. These were bitten into the plate, the etched areas deeply bitten in the acid bath. The plate was then inked and wiped with Sienna ink.

Then the wiped area was covered with a precut stencil paper. Five areas had been cut in the stencil which was fitted to register exactly with the etched plate. Five color spots were forced through the holes in the stencil and rolled on with gelatin rollers. These colors were also treated with gel to give them transparency.

Where the artist wished to have sharp whites on the print, pieces of metal, formed of malleable metal wire, were placed in strategic spots. The second plate was then ready and registered to print on the yellow area of the paper, and to be run through the etching press for the final print.

"Scylla and Charybdis," by Barbara Neustadt, Odyssey Series.
Courtesy of the Ruth White Gallery.

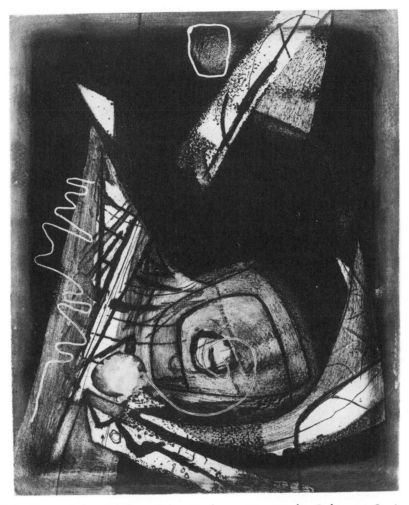

"Blinding of the Cyclops," by Barbara Neustadt, Odyssey Series.
Courtesy of the Ruth White Gallery.

This deeply bitten etching and aquatint was made with one plate, inked and wiped in four colors although it appears here in black and white. As in "The Lotus Eaters," the shaped areas of metal were placed on the plate in various positions to suit the artist's purpose. The metal disks were wiped in red and orange and printed accordingly. The plate was then run through the press.

In this print two plates were printed together on the bed of the press. Each plate was deep-bite etched and aquatinted. White areas were routed out by electric tool. Under pressure of the press rollers, they printed with a raised surface on the paper.

Plate 1 was inked and wiped with earth-green ink. After etching and aquatinting, Plate 2 was inked and wiped in blue-black ink. Other color areas in this type of print can be added at the discretion of the artist, using the same technique as that described in "The Lotus Eaters."

The variations of light in the color were obtained by additional wiping by hand, using the heel of the palm to pick up the ink.

The two plates were set together and run through the press.

Lillian Lent, who is director of the Graphic Workshop, Woodstock Artists' Association, and assistant at the Tyler School of Fine Arts, Temple University, makes beautiful soft-ground etchings by first laying a hard ground mixed with oil. She presses into the ground any textured material which suits her purpose: silk, leaves, cloth, string, sandpaper, or lace. The textured material picks up the soft ground, permitting the acid to bite into the plate to produce the texture. "Mulberries at Midnight," above, is a soft-ground etching entirely. The drawing on the soft-ground plate was made through a newspaper overlay.

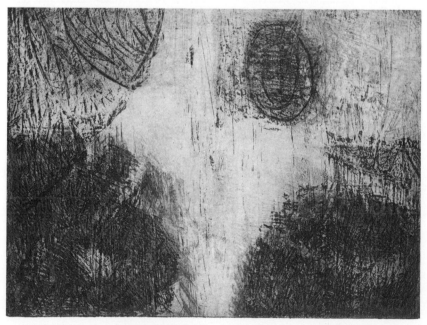

"Mulberries at Midnight," by Lillian Lent, intaglio etching, artist's proof, 1959. Courtesy of the artist.

Variety in Etching Technique

As you will see in the making of a number of etchings reproduced in these pages many effects are achieved by what would appear to be tricks of technique. I do not use the word trick in any disparaging way. Every method which furthers the creative ends of the artist is legitimate. The conventional tools of any medium may be supplemented by invented ones if the desired result is achieved.

Examine these offbeat additions to the conventional graphic methods, but use them sparingly and only after you have thoroughly practiced the classic procedures.

"Sleeping Bird Hill," by Lillian Lent. Artist's proof, 1963.

"Clown," by L. Calapai. Artist's proof.
Courtesy of the artist.

"Space Man," by L. Calapai. Artist's proof.

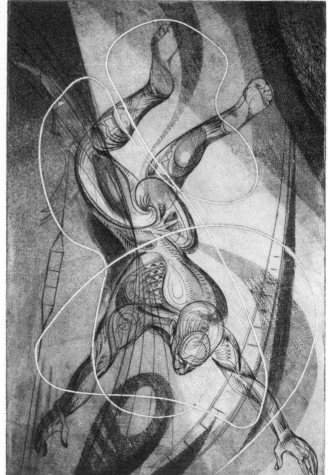

"Under the Big Top," by L. Calapai. Artist's proof.
Combined soft-ground etching, engraving, aquatint, and embossed white.

"Ascent and Descent," by L. Calapai. Artist's proof.
Engraving, soft-ground etching, and aquatint.

"Vulcan's Isle," by L. Calapai. Engraving and aquatint.

"Earthquake," by L. Calapai.
Color engraving and soft-ground etching.

Lithography

There is only one conventional planographic method—lithography, which is a surface printing technique. However, all impressions made by contact without using either the incised or raised line can properly be considered planographic. For instance, the technique described later under the name of "sensitypes" also belongs in this category.

Lithography is an extraordinary medium which is very popular with graphic artists. It is so beautiful that artists of every variety have at one time or another made a few prints by this method, even though they were pulled from the press by professional printers. The method is so ingenious that it must be included among the most creative inventions.

The process was discovered by a German named Aloys Senefelder in 1798. He took a simple principle—the natural antipathy of greasy substances for water—and applied it in the development of an art medium.

Briefly, the process is as follows: A thick, heavy piece of limestone, ground absolutely flat on its widest surface, serves as the receiver of the drawing. The drawing is made with greasy crayons directly on the polished surface of the porous limestone, which now has a fine grain.

After the drawing is completed, the entire surface is covered with a wash of water. Wherever the greasy crayon has touched, the water is repelled, so that only the undrawn areas are dampened.

A roller very similar to a baker's rolling pin, but capable of absorbing printer's ink, is saturated with the special greasy lithographic printing ink. It is then rolled over the damp stone surface, where it adheres only to the crayon lines of the drawing.

The printing is done by placing a dampened sheet of paper on the surface of the stone. When this is passed through the great pressure of the lithographic press scraper, the drawing on the stone is transferred to the paper faithfully, but as a reverse of the original.

Lithograph stones are heavy limestone blocks about three to four inches in thickness. When ground (with another stone and abrasives) the porous surface produced is ready to receive fine drawing lines and tones made with greasy crayons, pencils, or with tusche, a grease in liquid form.

The ground stone.

Lithograph tools.

White line. The use of a white incised
line to produce an image on the print.

Drawing on the Stone

A drawing is made on the delicately grained surface of a stone or zinc plate with a grease pencil or with an oily ink. When the surface is covered with a flow of water, the greased drawing will reject the water, which will remain on the other areas in a fine thin film, caught by the texture.

Drawing on the stone.

Tusche

Tusche is a variety of ink made of thinned, liquefied grease. This may be applied with a brush or even a pen upon the stone or zinc lithograph surface. It will have the same water-repellent quality as the grease crayon but will produce a print resembling a wash of black or grayed water color.

The lithograph roller, heavily impregnated with ink, is passed over the surface of the stone or plate. The water-covered area will reject the ink, the greased drawing will receive it.

The Lithograph Roller

The roller for inking the lithograph stone is leather-covered and when new requires steeping in a lithograph varnish in order to condition it properly to ink saturation. The varnish may be applied to the roller with the hand and worked into the leather. Then continue to work the varnish into the leather by rolling it many times over a clean slab of glass or marble.

When the leather is sufficiently soft and free of nap, steep it in fresh ink by many rollings. Then clean off the excess ink and set the roller on its handles, raised free of any contact and consequent damaging pressures.

The Lithograph Press

The lithograph press is designed for only one purpose: to draw a bar across the back of the dampened paper on the stone or zinc with such great pressure that the drawing is transferred from the stone to the paper in this one operation.

A smooth, shiny cardboard card larger than the stone or paper is used as a buffer between the delicate paper and the blunt pressure bar; this protects the paper from buckling under the heavy pressure. The stone and its paper and cardboard travel on a flat "bed" which moves on rollers under the fixed pressure bar. When this has been done the print is ready for removal from the stone.

The lithograph press. A high-pressure press with a scraper which passes over the stone or metal to transfer the image to paper.

Etching the Lithograph Stone

After you have made your drawing in lithographic pencils or tusche or both you are now prepared to take steps to see that this water-soluble drawing will not disappear when water is poured over the stone previous to the inking process.

The method of "fixing" the drawing so that it is impervious to the dissolving action of the water is called etching the stone. The name is somewhat confusing because what takes place is not in any way comparable to the "eating" process which occurs in metal-plate etching.

The etching of a drawing is achieved by flowing onto the stone a mixture of gum arabic dissolved in water with an addition of nitric acid. This very ingenious procedure "sets" the drawing upon the stone, making it waterproof.

The mixture is concocted as follows. A couple of ounces of gum arabic, which is sold in crystal form, are dissolved in enough water to give a gummy quality to the mixture. To this viscous mixture are added about fifty drops of nitric acid.

From your mixing glass pour some of the etch mixture onto the stone and spread it over the whole stone. (You may use the palm of your hand —the acid mixture is not strong enough to burn you; however, some prefer to use a brush for spreading.) After having covered the whole stone with the first pouring, give a second coating to the drawing area. Spread the etch to a very fine film before it gets too dry to handle. Now let it dry completely, and your stone is etched.

After the stone has been etched and has dried, it must be washed with turpentine. During this process the drawing will almost disappear. Don't let that frighten you. The etch has fixed it and the turpentine merely removes the blackness from the crayons leaving the greased areas of the drawing intact and ready to accept the ink and reject water.

Let the stone dry. Wash off the turpentine layer with clean water and a sponge. You are now ready for the inking and press.

Place the stone on the bed of the press. Charge the ink roller well with lithograph printing ink on the inking slab. Now sponge the stone with water. While it is quite wet all over roll on the ink. Ink the stone again and again until the drawing reappears in its original richness as you drew it. The ink, of course, has been rejected by all the areas of the stone other than the drawn, greased parts.

Printing Paper

Many types of paper are available for making etching and lithograph prints; the choice depends on the artist. The fact is that any good water-absorbent paper is adequate. Your art material dealer will offer a wide variety, so examine the papers used by other printmakers and choose the one you prefer.

Both for etching and lithography, the paper is ready for the press when it is faintly damp—not moist, and certainly never when soaking wet. The dampness must not be such as to reject the ink from the plate or stone but sufficient to make the paper pliable under pressure. One good method of insuring the right degree of dampness is to use a dampened blotter at the top and bottom of your sheets of paper. The dampness will permeate but not soak the paper.

Steps in Making a Lithograph

"Blind Man's Buff," by Tommy Beere. Rough sketch
on drawing paper made with lithograph crayon.

First proof.

An experiment in shadings and ink. Note the registry crosses. This is a time-honored printer's method of joining two "registered" overlays of color plates. Registry crosses in the margin area mark each detail section to be added. These must be so placed that they will exactly fit over similar crosses on the area beneath to insure correct alignment.

126

Another experiment in shading and ink.

Final decision. Finished print of "Blind Man's Buff."

Trial proof. John McClellan.

John McClellan

Print by John McClellan, 1961. Courtesy of artist.

John McClellan

The Silk-Screen Process

The silk-screen process is essentially a stenciling procedure. Ink or paint is forced through a fine fabric onto the surface of the print paper by the pressure of a tool called a squeegee. To distinguish the commercial silk-screening process from the fine handwork of the artist, the artist's product is called a serigraph.

Many printmakers of the orthodox school of graphic artists refuse to accept the serigraph as an authentic graphic art medium; but we take the position that artists do not paint according to rules nor do they make prints dictated by rules. Theirs is the business of creating art, and silk-screen prints can be very good art.

A piece of silk stretched taut on a wooden stretcher is the work surface. The silk, being porous, allows pigment to be forced through its fine mesh by pressure of a squeegee, which is a stick with a rubber edge, resembling a windshield wiper.

Areas not to be affected by the paint are blocked out on the silk with a stop-out solution. Paper placed beneath the screen of silk receives the color. Each color requires a separate screen.

The frame, or stretcher, for the silk screen should be sturdy and made so that it will lie flat on the paper. The corners should be weighted down with metal angle irons. Good silk-screen frames and work boxes are available in art supply shops and they are not expensive.

The frame should be hinged to a flat baseboard somewhat larger than its own size. Stretch the silk taut on the frame and staple it securely to the sides.

Commercially prepared stop-out solutions are available, or glue and water, mixed to a gummy, opaque covering will make a suitable substitute. When stop-out areas are to be removed, they may be washed off with cold water. The stop-out solution is painted on the silk in the areas which are not to receive color.

Pigments mixed to a creamy consistency are squeegeed across the screen and forced through the fine mesh only in the non-stopped areas. The silk may then be washed clean with cold water or it may be replaced with that used for the next color.

Some silk-screen artists use a cut-out stencil of paper, placed under the screen between it and the print paper. This takes the place of the stop-out method. The stencil may be pasted lightly to the underside of the screen.

Be sure that the paper which is to receive the second color is in proper position to "register" correctly with the first area of color.

During the printing process it is important that the screen frame be locked in place in relation to the baseboard so the design will print in correct position on the paper beneath. This may be done with two small hooks placed at each end of the frame.

Print by Anton Refregier. Courtesy of the artist.

"Mountain Monster," by Bernard Steffen.
Courtesy of the artist.

"Haying Time," by Bernard Steffen.

"Fodder Chopper," by Bernard Steffen.

"Autumn," by Bernard Steffen.

Silk screen print in color, by Karl Fortess.
Courtesy of the artist.

"Factory," by Karl Fortess.

138

Karl Fortess

139

Karl Fortess

Monotypes

A graphic method is, in the strictest sense, one in which a print is pulled from a source other than itself: It must come from a "matrix" or "mother" drawing or painting.

One of the popular graphic methods is the pulling of monotypes even though these are not identical. Each of the prints pulled from a matrix will be an approximation of the original; but each will have unique qualities quite beyond the control of the artist-printer. The monotype is an authentic medium, full of surprises, but it often yields interesting and satisfying results.

Every artist knows that there are elements which enter into each of his paintings that are not strictly within his control. The fluidity of his paints, effects of gravity on their flow, the spread of brush hairs, unplanned and reflex action of muscles—all produce accidental qualities which the artist seizes upon and utilizes to the benefit of his painting. In the case of monotypes, almost all the individuality is accidental.

The basic principle in making monotypes is that of contact. This is best demonstrated by the childhood game of making ink blot prints. An ink blot on one half of a piece of paper will produce a replica of itself on the other half if the paper is folded while the ink is still wet. Rorschach test blots are made this way. It required little imagination to adapt the technique to an orderly design; and even if it is composed of several colors a reasonable reverse facsimile can be readily achieved if the paper is folded while the ink is still damp.

Simple as the method is, it has been the source of extremely handsome prints. Some of the monotype makers use oil paints for the matrix. Owing to the convenient fact that the oil paints are extremely slow in drying, the time available to make a careful or complex matrix painting is considerable.

The transfer may be made hours after the oil painting is begun. Not so with most other media, parts of which would dry before the whole was finished and the resultant monotype print would be imperfect.

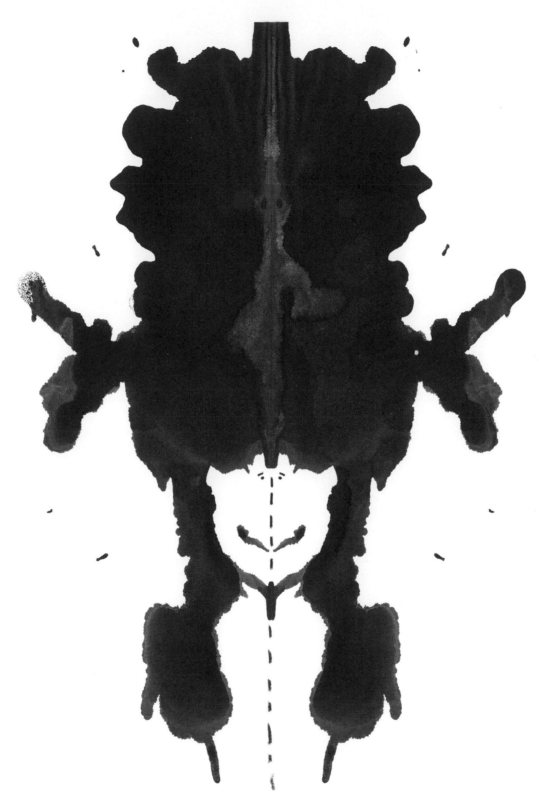

Inkspot print.

Drawing for monotype painting.

Monotype impression taken from painting on glass.

Faint second proof.

First sketch for painting on acetate.

Matrix painting for monotype print made on acetate instead of glass.

Monotype print made from acetate.

Matrix painting on acetate for monotype.

Monotype print from acetate.

New Methods of Printmaking

Printmakers living at the time of Aloys Senefelder's invention of the lithographic process must have been outraged at the pretensions of that extremely "different" medium. Until that fateful year of 1798, the artists who produced prints were limited to engraving and etching on wood or on copper or other metal. I am sure the lithographic method was looked upon as an intrusion of the "machine age" at that time and considered unworthy of the purist's attention. Certainly the resulting prints were of small monetary value to the collectors of the period.

Respectability almost invariably comes with age, and as each new "art machine" comes into being, the die-hards of orthodoxy seek means to discredit or at least disparage the purity of the product of these new gadgets.

The demand for quality and faithfulness is a most reasonable and worthy one. Obstinate opposition to the new and daring is another matter. The print collector, if he is an antiquarian, is quite right to shun all but the authentically old, the "first edition," and the numbered, severely limited printing from the unretouched plate. If he is an investor with an eye on a select, precious market, he is doubly and shrewdly right. But orthodoxy has always fought a losing battle, and where it has sought to impede the daring and invention of the artist it has invariably found itself, although well entrenched, flanked and bypassed by creators strangely indifferent to these last-ditch defenders.

Special Effects

Along with the innovations in all the arts, a spirit of experimentation and irreverence for conventions has developed and now pervades the graphic-art field. Woodcutters are using metal screening tapped into the surface with a hammer to register patterns. This has also been used effectively on copper and zinc plates.

Some artists use hand electric drills, employing various routers, roulettes, sanders, and multiple-toothed cutters set in the chuck of the drill to obtain textures and designs unobtainable by hand cutting.

Three-dimensional prints are made by soldering wire twisted into desired designs onto the plate surface. These raised patterns are pressed into heavy dampened paper, which is then dried, and the design is set in the paper in intaglio.

Collages glued upon the block surface "print" a three-dimensional impression. In making these collages any amount of inventiveness is permissible: Burlap, corrugated metal, marble dust, or wood shavings are often used effectively.

Plaster and plastic wood are also frequently used for both intaglio and cameo as well as uninked, three-dimensional impressions.

A porous ground on a metal plate may be obtained by sprinkling salt on the still-soft warm ground. When dry and hard the plate may be immersed in water and the salt will dissolve, leaving tiny pockmarks in the ground which will produce a halftone value on the print. This is called salt printing.

Many other materials are employed to achieve results similar but not identical to those obtained in conventional printmaking. Plywood, wallboard, Plexiglass, and porous stone, to name but a few, have been used to good effect.

Chemigraphs

In this process a light-box is used in connection with a paper covered with a light-sensitive coating. Many such papers are produced, but I have found the Kodak Verifax Fine Line paper most effective.

A light-box is simple to construct as shown on pp. 152 and 153. In addition to this, you will need the following:

Verifax activator diluted in water to varying degrees depending on the value desired (greater dilution makes for lighter tones).
A plastic or glass pan for the activating liquid.
An electric hot plate for warming the activating liquid.
A squeegee made of rubber or sponge to wipe off the excess activator liquid.

Photographic blotting paper or any lint-free bond paper to help draw off excess activator fluid.

The procedure in making chemigraphs is as follows:

1. Make a drawing in strong black-and-white contrast.

2. On the curved Fiberglass surface of the light-box, place a sheet of Verifax Fine Line (coated face up) as matrix.

3. Place your drawing face down on the matrix paper. (Remember, the *matrix* will be the final print.)

4. Cover the joined drawing and matrix and turn on the lights in the light-box. Expose the drawing to the matrix for approximately twenty seconds.

5. Remove the matrix from the light-box and immerse it in the activator liquid warmed to about 75 to 80° F. on the hot plate. If the activator solution is too hot or too cold the results will not be good.

6. Remove the matrix from the activator and cover with lint-free bond paper or photographers' blotters.

7. Use squeegee with moderate pressure on the back of the paper or blotter to absorb the excess activator fluid.

8. Gently peel the paper (or blotter) from the matrix and, still very gently, wipe the matrix with a soft cloth or another squeegee.

9. When the matrix is dry, expose it to the sun's action to bring out inherent colors. You will now have produced a toned variation bearing only a slight similarity to the black and white of your basic drawing. The matrix will be in hues of tan or brown or yellows, depending on the strength of the activator solution, the time of exposure to the sun, and the sun's strength.

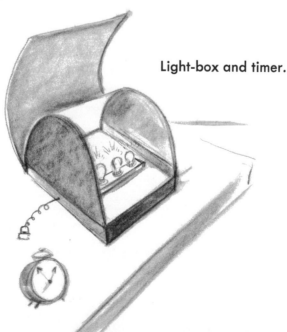

Light-box and timer.

10. If you wish to touch up your matrix print with additional drawing details the surface is ideal for scratch drawing with a razor blade or any sharp tool very much in the manner of a drypoint.

11. For each matrix print to be pulled from your drawing the complete process described above must be repeated.

The procedure for making chemigraphs may strike you as a mechanical one, but as you experiment with activator strength, time of immersion in the liquid, time of exposure in the sun (and its variation in strength), you will develop skills in guiding your matrix print to produce hues and tones you wish stressed.

It is a method not very much more mechanical than lithography and a valid graphic process on its own.

Activator in gallon jug.

Activator in pan for printing.

Original drawing.

Print made on light-box with additional hand "scratching."

A second print made on light-box with longer time exposure.

"Kyoto," original drawing by the author.

"Kyoto," reverse chemigraph print on matrix.

Second chemigraph print, from matrix to matrix.

Sensitypes

I have given the name "sensitype" to a new method of making two almost identical contact prints, because light and chemical sensitivity are important ingredients in the process.

There are many light-sensitive photographic papers on the market and experimentation with a number of them is suggested, although here, however, I shall outline the method and materials which I have used for some years, producing prints of many colors and of relative permanence.

The paper I use is a Kodak product, Verifax Fine Line Matrix. This paper is a relatively slow developer and drawings can be executed upon its smooth surface in a not too sunny room in a leisurely manner, though it must be completed in one "sitting."

The drawing may be made in pencil. A solution of Verifax activator used diluted in cold water is applied with a brush to produce the dark brown and near black lines and other dark areas of the drawing. The tonal intensity will vary with the amount of dilution; the less the dilution, the darker the tone.

Photographer's fixing solution (I use FR Develochrome) is used at this stage to produce ivory whites. These whites will scarcely show against the white of the paper, but as the remainder of the paper, unexposed to the chemicals, is exposed to sunlight it will turn reddish brown, and the ivory whites will be strongly revealed.

Before the paper is exposed to the sun, while still in your shaded studio (a dark room is not necessary, merely sunless) and after you have painted the black-brown areas and the ivory white ones, you must proceed with the making of a contact-monotype pulled from your present drawing while still wet.

Place another sheet of Verifax Fine Line paper face down against the wet drawing. Do not rub it hard against the drawing; merely allow its weight to take the imprint.

Gently pull the two sheets apart after one minute of contact. The second sheet will have picked up sufficient chemical from the first to reproduce a similar drawing, in reverse, on its coated surface.

Now expose both sheets of paper to sunlight. As you watch, the areas of the paper untouched by chemical brush strokes will react to the light, changing color. Allow this action to continue until the background color satisfies your taste.

Remove from sunlight and "fix." I use clear plastic spray from a can for this.

Unless exposed to excessive further powerful sunlight the two almost identical prints will remain permanent. This is true of almost all drawings, paintings, and prints. Overexposure to very strong sun will fade and change original color.

Should you wish to add areas of color to the two drawings the Develochrome will act upon the sun-developed areas of red-brown and deep red, producing a strong yellow.

Clear water applied to the chemically produced ivory white areas will produce soft blue tints. These in turn must be sprayed with the clear plastic.

Contact duotype of bird made with sensitype method, first matrix.

Same, contact matrix.

Contact duotype of horse and rider made
with sensitype method, first matrix.

Same, contact matrix.

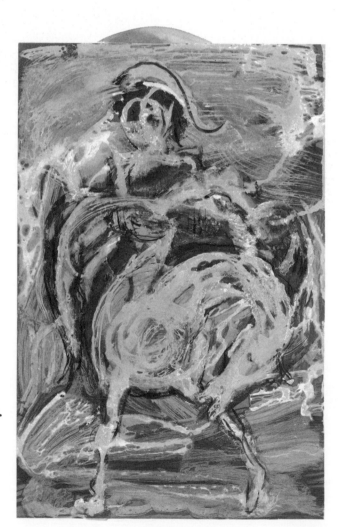

Contact duotype of mother and child made
with sensitype method, first matrix.

Same, contact matrix.

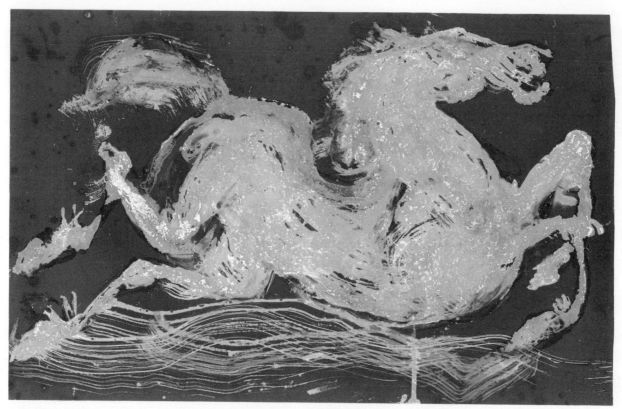

Monotype of stallion, using sensitype method.

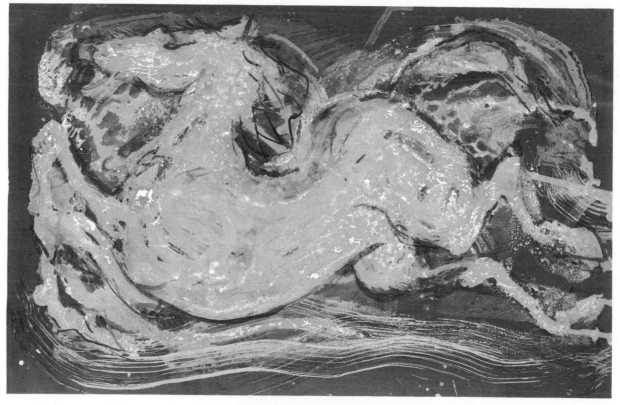

Same, contact matrix.

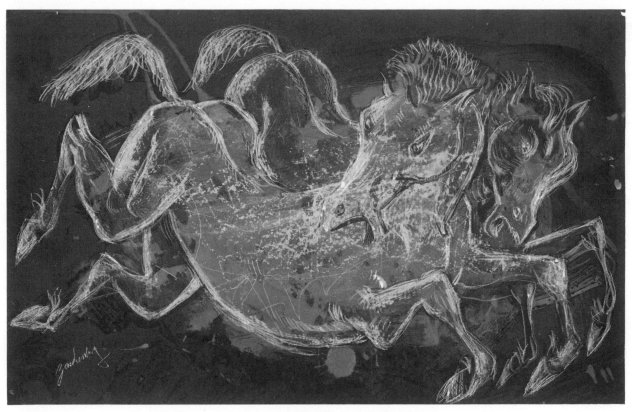

Matrix

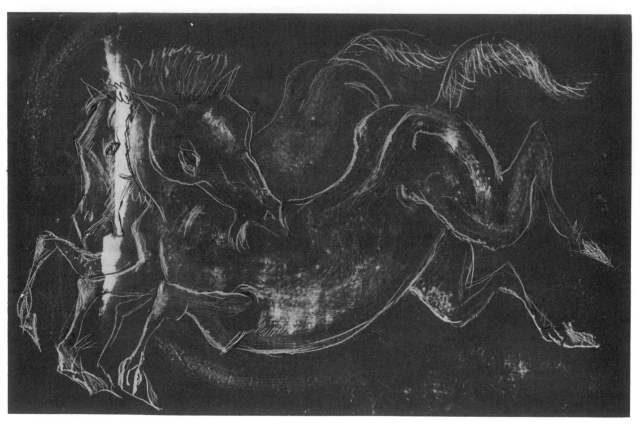

Print 1

Wild Stallions—Matrix

Wild Stallions—Print 2

Three faces

Glossary

AQUATINT—An etching medium which allows halftone values to be bitten on the plate through porous ground.

ASPHALTUM—A variety of varnish used for "stopping out" areas on the etching plate which have been sufficiently bitten.

BATH—The liquid used for the acid bath. Any material which is acid-proof will serve (glass, porcelain, etc.) as a container.

BEVEL—The slope of the edge of the etching plate, made so that the plate will not cut the paper under pressure of the press rollers.

BITING—The acid action of the bath on the metal plate.

BLANKET—The felt pads used between the press rollers and the plate and paper to relieve pressure.

BOXWOOD—A hard wood used by wood engravers for wood-block cutting and engraving.

BRAYER—The printmaker's name for the leather- or rubber-covered roller used for inking plates and grounding plates with wax or varnish for etching.

BURIN—A cutting tool for engraving on wood or metal.

BURNISHER—A rounded steel tool for removing or reducing etched lines on a plate.

BURR—The metal ridges formed by the cutting edge of the drypoint needle. It may be removed with a tool or left on the plate. It produces soft, furry lines in printing.

CARBORUNDUM—An abrasive used for graining a stone for lithography.

CLICHÉ VERRE—A process of making prints using a glass sheet covered with an opaque coat. When scratched with a sharp point, the exposed lines may be printed on light sensitized photographic paper and then fixed.

DABBER—A pad of silk or leather used to "push" printing ink into etched lines. It may also be used as a ground-laying aid for the etching plates.

DAMPENING—The moistening of batches of paper in preparation for printing from plate or stone.

DIAMOND TOOL—A drypoint tool tipped with an industrial diamond chip.

DRYPOINT—The graphic process in which lines are scratched into the copper or zinc plates with a sharp tool rather than bitten by acids.

DUTCH MORDANT—An acid mixture for biting etching plates. It is composed of hydrochloric acid and potassium chlorate.

END-GRAIN WOOD—The hardwood blocks used for fine engraving. The grain runs at right angles to the working surface.

ENGRAVING—The process of cutting a line or incised area into a plate or wood block.

ETCHING—The graphic printmaking process which uses acids to bite incised areas on a metal plate.

ETCHING TOOL—The pointed metal tool used to penetrate the ground on a plate to expose the metal for acid action.

FEATHER—Used as an aid for spreading acid on limited areas of the etching plate.

GEL—A commercially prepared jelly to mix with paint or ink to enhance transparency.

GRAIN—The subtle "tooth," or surface texture, of a lithograph stone prepared for drawing.

GROUND—The covering film on an etching plate which resists the action of acids. Varnishes, waxes, or resins are used as a film.

HEATER—A hot plate for warming metal plates for applying ground and for inking.

IMPRESSION—The image printed from a stone, plate, wood block, or any other matrix.

INK—The special printing ink used for rolling on the plate, stone, or block. It is sold in tubes at art supply shops.

INKING PLATE—A flat sheet of glass, stone, or metal used in saturating the ink roller or dabber with printer's ink.

LINOLEUM BLOCK—Any good quality linoleum used for cutting in the process similar to making a woodcut. The printing surface is in relief.

LITHOGRAPHY—The process of making prints from drawings made on stone or on metal sheets, using the water-repellent properties of greasy inks as a basic principle.

LITHOGRAPH CRAYONS—Greasy crayons and pencils for drawing on stone or metal.

LITHOGRAPH PRESS—A high-pressure press which draws a scraper across the paper, transferring the image from stone or metal to the paper.

LITHOGRAPH STONES—Heavy limestone blocks about 3 to 4 inches in thickness. When ground (with another stone and abrasives) the porous surface produced is ready to receive fine drawing lines and tones made with greasy crayons or pencils, or with tusche, a liquefied grease.

MEZZOTINTS—A process of intaglio printmaking. The printing surface of the plate is "rocked" with a special tool which gives halftone tints to the prints obtained.

MONOTYPE—A method of pulling one reverse facsimile of a painting made upon a hard surface (glass, porcelain, or metal) by superimposing a sheet of paper and rubbing the reverse side until the image is transferred.

NITRIC ACID—A biting agent most commonly used in etching. It is also used (in a mixture with gum arabic) for etching lithograph drawings on the stone.

PLANOGRAPHIC METHODS—Printmaking devices whereby the print is obtained from the flat surface of the plate, stone, or any other matrix.

PLATE MARK—The impression in the paper left by the pressure of the plate edges.

PROOF—A preliminary impression pulled for examination of various stages until the final stage is reached.

PULLING—The action of printing from the matrix onto the paper.

REGISTER—The process of fitting two or more plates together to print in required position.

RELIEF—The raised surface which is the source of the image in relief processes.

RESIN—A substance, granulated to form a porous film, that can be used as a ground for aquatints.

ROCKER—A steel tool shaped to allow its many teeth to bite into the plate surface as it is rocked. It produces a textured surface.

ROULETTE—A toothed wheel used to make tiny perforations in the ground or on the plate surface in etching and drypoint.

RUBBING—The process of pulling a print from an inked matrix. It is also the name for pulling a facsimile from a bas-relief sculpture. The paper is placed against the clear sculptured surface and its back is rubbed with a flat-edged crayon or pencil. The image appears un-reversed on the paper.

SALT PRINTING—A method of producing a halftone value by sprinkling salt on the still-soft warm ground. When dry and hard, the plate may be immersed in water and the salt will dissolve, leaving tiny pockmarks.

SCRAPING TOOL—A sharp three-edged tool used for shaving the un-wanted burr thrown up by the drypoint tool.

SERIGRAPH—The graphic process wherein stencils arc uscd. The silk-screen process is referred to by artists as serigraph printing. In this process inks or paints are forced through a fine silk mesh by the use of a "squeegee."

SOFT GROUND—An etching ground softened and made porous so that the acid will bite through, giving special textures to the etching.

SQUEEGEE—The rubber-edged blade, much like a windshield wiper, used to force ink or paint through a silk stencil in making serigraph prints.

STOPPING OUT—The process of blocking off areas sufficiently bitten from further action of the acid, by the use of stopping-out varnish.

TARLETAN—A mesh rag used for wiping excess ink from the metal-plate surface after the ink has been forced into the incised lines.

TUSCHE—Liquefied grease used with a brush on lithograph stones.

WASHING WITH TURPENTINE—The process of removing the grease crayon drawing from a stone.

WHITE LINE—The white incised line used to produce an image on the print.

WHITING—A powder which, mixed with water, forms a cleansing paste to be used on plate surfaces before laying the ground.

WOODCUT—One of the relief graphic processes. The areas to appear in ink on the paper print are those which are left in relief on the sur-face, in contrast to the cut-away areas. Woodcuts are made on plank or flat-grained wood.

WOOD ENGRAVING—This is also a relief process and, because the work is often very fine, with minute lines, end-grain wood is used.

ABOUT THE AUTHOR

Arthur Zaidenberg was born in Brooklyn, New York, in 1903. As a young man he studied art at the National Academy in New York, the Beaux Arts in Paris, the Kunstakademie in Munich, and the American Academy in Rome.

Throughout his career his interests have ranged widely in the arts. He has instructed in drawing at New York University. He has written many books about various aspects of art. He has illustrated books, notably editions of *Candide, Thaïs, Against the Grain, Beatrice Cenci,* and the Fine Editions Club edition of *Plays of William Shakespeare.* He is reputed to have painted more murals in the United States than any other painter. He has practiced in many different media, and his work is included in the collections of the Metropolitan Museum of Art and other museums and galleries and in private collections.

Mr. Zaidenberg has a wide reputation as painter, teacher, lecturer, and author. He lives in Woodstock, New York, and travels frequently.